Sharon Pollock
Three Plays

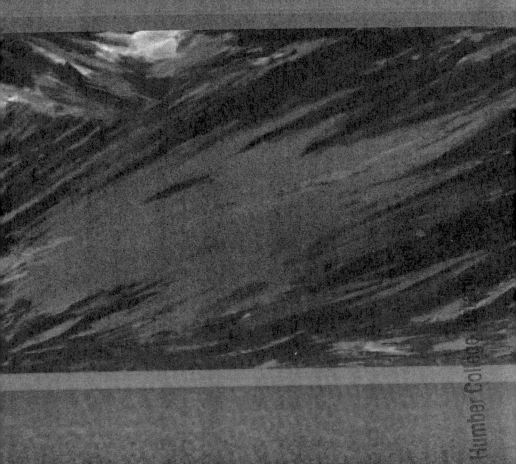

Sharon Pollock
Three Plays

Introductory essay by Sherrill Grace.

Playwrights Canada Press
Toronto•Canada

Playwrights Canada Press
54 Wolseley Street, 2nd Floor, Toronto, Ontario CANADA M5T 1A5
416-703-0013   fax 416-703-0059
orders@playwrightscanada.com • www.playwrightscanada.com

Playwrights Canada Press acknowledges the support of the taxpayers of Canada and the province of Ontario through The Canada Council for the Arts and the Ontario Arts Council.

Cover painting "Kythera 1999" by Rita Letendre. 183 x 305 cm or 72 by 120 inches.
Production Editor/Cover Design: Jodi Armstrong

National Library of Canada Cataloguing in Publication

Pollock, Sharon
  Sharon Pollock : three plays / introductory essay by Sherrill Grace.

Contents: Moving pictures — End dreams — Angel's trumpet.
ISBN 0-88754-656-0

  1. Shipman, Nell, 1892-1970—Drama. 2. Murder—British Columbia—Vancouver—Drama. 3. Vancouver (B.C.)—Race relations—Drama. 4. Fitzgerald, F. Scott (Francis Scott), 1896-1940—Drama. 5. Fitzgerald, Zelda, 1900-1948—Drama. I. Title. II. Title: Three plays. III. Title: Moving pictures. IV. Title: End dreams. V. Title: Angel's trumpet.

PS8581.O34S53 2003   C812'.54   C2003-901898-9
PR9199.3.P57S53 2003 ISBN

First edition: May 2003.
Printed and bound by AGMV Marquis at Quebec, Canada.

TABLE OF CONTENTS

— — • — • — —

THE ART OF SHARON POLLOCK
by Sherrill Grace
— — • — — • — —

In 1948 a British movie hit the cinemas and became an instant popular success. It was called "The Red Shoes." Moira Shearer starred in the role of the ballerina, Victoria Page, who was forced to choose between her career as a famous artist and her marriage to the man she loved. Loosely based on Hans Christian Andersen's fairytale *The Red Shoes*, the moral of the movie—for a generation of women who had joined the work force after the war and for their young daughters—was that women *shall not* be artists, and that if they aspire to artistic careers they will be destroyed by the very art they love. Those red shoes symbolize art, ambition, discipline, professional commitment, desire, and, of course, female sexuality, but in the movie they dance Victoria Page to her death beneath the wheels of a train. As Rosemary Sullivan reminds us in her biography of Margaret Atwood, *The Red Shoes: Margaret Atwood Starting Out*, a whole generation of girls saw that film, but not every girl was crushed into denying her artistic ambition and creative talent (4). Some of those girls put on the red shoes and lived to write about it.[1]

Not only are the three plays—published here for the first time—written by one of the great artists of the red shoes generation, but they are also, to varying degrees, about the telling of stories, about being women, and, especially, about being artists. Moreover, as you read these plays you will find more than passing reference to movies, shoes, and the colour red. With the prescience I have come to recognize and value in Pollock's work, she has created three challenging, uncompromising, and innovative plays that make powerful theatre out of public and private events that shape, condition or, at the very least, touch us all. These plays are firmly rooted in the soil of 20th century North American history, culture, and politics, but all three dance free from specific realities of time and place to find us where we live today.

Moving Pictures, based on the life and autobiography of the actress and independent silent filmmaker Nell Shipman, dramatizes the artist's painful struggle to make sense of her life and of her failure to survive the ruthless politics and economic monopolies of the emerging Hollywood studio system. *End Dream* returns to the hot summer of July 1924 in Vancouver's wealthy Shaughnessy Heights to re-open the infamous, unsolved case of Janet Smith, the English nanny found dead in her employer's basement. Janet is no artist, but the reliving of her story opens old wounds and a host of stories that society, even today, would like to forget. And *Angel's Trumpet* revisits the story of Zelda and Scott Fitzgerald to pose some of the same questions that inform many of Pollock's earlier plays: What does it take to be an artist and what are the costs to the artist and those around him or her? Of what does one make art and are there any ethical limits to the creative grasp? Can one be a woman, a wife, a mother *and* a successful artist? But possibly most disturbing of all – is art worth its price and, if so, why?

All three plays centre on an individual woman who finds herself trapped by contemporary socio-political power structures that are controlled by men, and all three have stunning roles for women. The male roles present other kinds of challenges. With the partial exception of Scott in *Angel's Trumpet*, men play peripheral and often threatening roles, but when I say peripheral I do not mean merely minor. Most of the men operate at the margins, from where they observe the action, pull the strings, maintain authority and control, while Scott performs as a would-be puppet-master who fights to control centre court in a marital squash game of life and death. All three plays are drawn from historical events and the recorded lives of real people; they are based on the research that Pollock so often undertakes for her work. In this respect, they remind me of *Walsh, The Komagata Maru Incident, Blood Relations, Saucy Jack,* and *Fair Liberty's Call.* But Pollock is never restricted by this research or tied down by the facts, which inform rather than dictate her vision. Thus, in *Moving Pictures* Nell Shipman achieves a self-knowledge that the real woman probably never achieved; in *End Dream* Janet Smith, the one person whose voice was never recorded—who was indeed a non-entity until she died—gets to speak; and in *Angel's Trumpet* Zelda puts her case with such power that *we*—her audience, listeners, readers—are forced to reconsider many of the myths and legends we hold dear; if we refuse her (and Pollock's) challenge, then it is *we* who will have had the experience but entirely missed the meaning.

Finally, in each of these plays Pollock experiments with form and structure, pushes the limits of what the theatre can do, and finds exciting answers to performance questions about representing, in the physical, embodied language of the stage, the subjective truths of personal experience, the inner struggles of characters searching for meaning in their lives, and the private traumas of betrayal, exploitation, failure, madness, and despair. To be sure, Pollock has always pushed her craft by experimenting with formal responses to the demands of the theatre. When the time arrives to assess how her art has changed over the years from *Walsh* to *End Dream,* for example, or from *Blood Relations* to *Moving Pictures,* or from *Getting It Straight* to *Angel's Trumpet,* I predict that we will find a sustained beauty of language across her œuvre, a formal development in the honing of craft, but also a deepening of vision that is fully integrated with performance – an exquisite balance of the literary and the theatrical. It is a cliché, I know, but in these plays the medium is the message, as it is in *Blood Relations, Doc,* or *Fair Liberty's Call,* and these new plays have a great deal to offer the innovative designer, as well as actors and directors, for Pollock knows better than most playwrights, not just how profoundly a play exists on stage, but how to write *for the stage.*[2]

Moving Pictures

Moving Pictures premiered with Calgary's Theatre Junction on 10 March 1999 at the Dr. Betty Mitchell Theatre under the direction of Brian Richmond, with set and lighting design by Terry Gunvordahl, and with Shawna Burnett, Thea Gill, and Lory Wainberg as the three phases of the heroine. It is based on the life of Canadian-born actress, film star, and filmmaker Nell Shipman (1892-1970) whose autobiography, *The Silent Screen & My Talking Heart* (1987), provided Pollock with the facts of her protagonist's life but also with a subjective, partial narrative *against* which her play functions. And this point is important: Pollock has said that, in her view, the Nell Shipman of the autobiography failed to grasp the socio-political and economic realities of her world.[3] Although Shipman remained true to her artistic vision—to create movies that explored human relations within a healing, natural world using wild and domestic animals without subjecting them to cruelty—she seemed unaware of the public politics that shaped her or that her own æsthetic stance had a politic. In short, the real Shipman did not *get it,* whereas Pollock's Shipman does. Where the real Shipman pushed the forces of patriarchy to the margins of her autobiography, Pollock places them on stage, always there, observing, commenting on, and controlling the parameters of the woman's life. Key amongst these male powers-that-be is Thomas Edison who created *moving* pictures by harnessing the persistence of vision that makes illusion seem real, and Pollock stages Edison as a presiding voice-over impressario whom we, and Shipman, cannot afford to ignore.

In her note on the text, Pollock explains that the play "explores the meaning of story-telling in our lives, and the artist's addiction to creation whatever the cost" (2). This comment provides important clues to the play's structure and its themes because *Moving Pictures* is both a memory play and a portrait of the *woman* artist who, near the end of her life, must try to understand the choices she made and the meaning of her life as an artist. To reach this understanding, "Shipman" will relive her life with the help of "Helen," her young, ingenue-self, and "Nell," her mature, filmmaker-self. But the memories shaped by a story-telling that will construct her life and produce its meaning do not come easily. The elderly "Shipman" has just received a letter informing her of a terminal illness; she is bitter, alone, angry, accusatory, and afraid. But her younger selves are less ready to give up. "Nell" and "Helen" pester "Shipman" to make something of this bad news by commanding her to "Play!" At first the old woman refuses, but as she gradually sees what her younger selves are making of her life she moves in: this is Shipman's life after all. *She* is its central figure and it is she who has lived through what the others are—as far as she's concerned— sugar-coating.

The dramatic tension that propels this play develops in steadily increasing waves as the characters jockey for control of the story-telling process. The result is an emotional tug-of-war that never lets up. Whenever "Helen" or "Nell" attempt to gloss over the traumas of the past, "Shipman" forces them to face some extremely painful truths – that she ignored her mother's self-sacrifice, abandoned her father and son to make her signature film *Back to God's Country* (1919), failed to understand the business end of her work, exploited the men in her personal life without appreciating the degree to which her world was conditioned by public men in power, and that she stubbornly subjected others (including her beloved animals) to her single-minded pursuit of art. The charge is that Nell Shipman was addicted to art and sacrificed everything to its service. The verdict enacted on stage is that she must relive her life, retell it, to see if the end justifies the means. But Pollock is too consummate an artist to hand us an unequivocal answer, and perhaps such an answer (if one exists) is beside the point. The meaning of this play, I think, is that an unexamined life is an unlived one and that, if you are an artist, you have a duty to search for meaning. Moreover, if your art is the theatre and you are a playwright, then your duty is to represent that search on stage in such a way as to make an audience feel and reflect upon what a life can mean, on the function of art, and on the often impossible choices all of us, including the artist, must make.

Absolutely inseparable from Pollock's creation of Shipman's life is the fact that Nell Shipman was a female artist. Thus, it is important for readers and audiences to ask why Pollock, at this stage in her career, chose this subject and to consider whether the benefit of her own late 20th century experience has helped her appreciate the dilemmas faced by an early 20th century woman in Shipman's profession. I think these questions are highly relevant and that Pollock's own position—as well as her art—has enabled her to write with unflinching honesty and courage about the *problems* of being not just an artist but a female artist. I would go further and predict that this play will provide many answers to the careful reader and, above all, to a live audience through a good production. One of those answers is "never!" Never give up, never stop asking the hard questions, never conform to conventions (social, sexual, or æsthetic), never betray your vision, and, most important, never disregard your relationships with others and your place in a complex social context. Pay attention to the voice-overs because they condition, finally, the basis of your humanity, without which you will never be an artist and never deserve to wear the red shoes of art.

End Dream
────•────•────

For the subject of this play Pollock has chosen one of those watershed moments in the formation of Canadian identity, much as she did with *Walsh*, *The Komagata Maru Incident*, and *Fair Liberty's Call*. And in some respects *End Dream* recalls these plays. The story is not much remembered today, but in 1924 Vancouver it was both sensational and highly political. When a young Scots nursemaid, Janet Smith (1902-24), was found dead in the basement of her wealthy employers' home, the Chinese houseboy quickly became a suspect. The newspapers went wild. Rumours of drug dealing, drunken parties, rape, and torture filled the headlines. Psychics were reported to have *dreamed* the scene of her death; police, coroners, journalists, lawyers, the Attorney-General, and members of elite families were accused of incompetence, cover-ups, crime, and abuse. The rhetoric of racism dominated much of the debate surrounding the case. In fact, Janet Smith's death became a lightning rod for an anti-Asian hysteria that lay close to the surface in the "white" Vancouver of the period. Only a decade had passed since the *Komagata Maru* was blocked from landing its Sikh passengers on Canadian soil; Asians born in this country were not citizens and could not vote; a "head" tax made immigration extremely difficult, and Caucasian women and Asian men were forbidden to work in the same public places. In another fifteen years Japanese Canadians living on the west coast would discover how quickly such racism could be mobilized.

We still do not know whether Janet Smith was murdered or committed suicide, although it seems unlikely that she killed herself. If she was murdered, then the murderer got away. The Chinese houseboy, Wong Foon Sing, who was kidnapped and tortured, then arrested, jailed, tried but acquitted, never changed his story about what he knew, and while some continued to suspect that he knew more than he divulged, he suddenly returned to China in March 1926 and disappeared. A full forensic examination of Smith's body could not be conducted, even when the corpse was disinterred and the inquiry re-opened, because it had been embalmed and buried without a proper autopsy. Key records from 1920-23 linking an international drug ring with the case, were sealed by Scotland Yard until 2001. In other words, despite investigations and a trial, a host of conflicting details, a number of possible suspects, and a potential motive, the clues were destroyed or covered up.

Because unsolved mysteries continue to tantalize, this one has inspired several literary treatments. The chief source for Pollock was Edward Starkins' *Who Killed Janet Smith?* But writers as different as Sky Lee and Frank Jones have also explored the subject—Lee in her award-winning novel *Disappearing Moon Café* (1990) and Jones in his pot-boiler collection of Canadian murder stories called *Trail of Blood*—and at least one other play (as yet unpublished) has been attempted.[4] Where *End Dream* differs from these other texts is in its richly layered orchestration of all the resources of theatre to bring Janet Smith back to life as the person through whose eyes the story must be told.

When the play opened for its world premiere on 8 March 2000 in its Calgary Theatre Junction production, Sharon Pollock was directing with a set and light design by Gunvordahl on the Betty Mitchell stage, and the combination was just right. *End Dream* demands a lot from everyone; it is, I think, one of the most technically and formally challenging of Pollock's works. The historical facts of the case might lead a director, designer, and cast to aim for realism and solutions, but such an approach would entirely miss both the point of the play and the challenge of performance because this is a dream play in which Janet Smith is conjured up to speak to us, to try to tell us why she died, and to shed some light on the barely submerged violence of life in the house where she worked and on the intrigue surrounding her in the new world society of Vancouver. If you want to know whodunit, you will be disappointed – as was at least one critic reviewing the play (see Creery). But if you want to plunge into a threatening dreamscape to imagine what it must have felt like to be surrounded by hints of crime and corruption, trapped by a ruthless man, who has hired you and paid your passage to Canada, to whom you are in debt and from whom you cannot escape, and subject to the unpredictable attentions of his jealous, alcoholic wife, then you will find this play a *tour de force*.

In an interview about the play, Pollock explained that she is "only interested in historical things if [she] can manipulate them." As she put it – "I want to make something bigger than the mystery" (see Kate Taylor R5). These kinds of comments are always relevant with Pollock, but they are especially so for *End Dream*. It is crucial to pay close attention to her stage instructions, to sound effects, lighting, and above all to the use of the stage. Space is one of the most powerful tools at Pollock's disposal here and the use she makes of the physical/visual potential of movement and stasis, of the proxemics of actors' bodies in relation to furniture or translucent walls, of mirroring effects, and especially of centre/margin tension make for drama that is intense, dynamic, and, in my experience, galvanizing. Whether reader or spectator, one is made complicit by virtue of looking, but the psychic distance between observer/ observed is slowly destroyed by the centripetal power of the play until pulling back, across whatever safe line of demarcation exists between here and there, self and other, is no longer possible. We are forced to enter Janet's world, Janet's troubled mind, Janet's confused, partial understanding of the corruption and prejudice around her just as she is forced to recognize her closest ally in the houseboy, who she formerly held in contempt as racially inferior and socially beneath her.

But I cannot reveal more of what happens. Suffice it to say that no one *in* the play is without suspicion or free of the social constraint and prejudice (of class, race, and gender) in the larger world beyond the boundaries of the play. However, I must touch on a key intertext in this complex play – the story of the red shoes. Part way into Act 2, there is a long scene between Janet and the wife, Doris, in which Doris asks for her shoes.[5] She suspects Janet of stealing them; Janet insists they are lost. When Janet finds "a pair of red shoes," Doris asks Janet to recite the story of the red shoes, and when the poor girl cannot (or will not), Doris does. The scene is utterly chilling, not least because when the story is finished Janet will put on the red shoes and…. But you must read the play.

Angel's Trumpet

Angel's Trumpet? A dictionary will tell you that "angel's-trumpet" is a flowering, solanaceous plant of the genus *Datura*, *D. arborea* or *D. suavolens* with large, trumpet-shaped flowers. What a dictionary will not explain (unless you dig) is that this flower is night-blooming, that it belongs to the deadly nightshade family, along with henbane and belladonna, and that it can be grown in the American South. No dictionary will tell you that it was one of Zelda Sayre Fitzgerald's favourite flowers or that she was an accomplished painter of lilies, peonies, and angel's-trumpets. When Sharon Pollock chose this title for her play about Zelda and Scott Fitzgerald, she did so with care, and any reading of the play should keep that sinister, beautiful, symbolic title in mind.

Unlike Tennessee Williams' play about the Fitzgeralds, *Clothes for a Summer Hotel: A Ghost Play* (1980), *Angel's Trumpet* does not try to recreate an era in American literary culture.[6] Instead of bringing the Fitzgeralds' friends, foes, lovers, and literary rivals on stage, as does Williams, Pollock zeros in on what I can only describe as the most quintessentially horrifying, but defining, *scene* in the real lives of this spectacularly stagey couple. From this concentrated and intensely focussed actual event, she creates a play as moving as and more frightening than *Doc, Getting It Straight,* or *Saucy Jack.* Once again, Pollock directed the play for its February 2001 premiere on the Betty Mitchell stage with Gunvordahl in charge of design. Reviews were positive, with critics reaching for comparisons with Ibsen's *A Doll's House* or Albee's *Who's Afraid of Virginia Woolf* (see Morrow).

The action starts on 28 May, 1933; the place is La Paix, an elegant house on a country estate near Towson, Maryland, which the Fitzgeralds had rented. The flapper exploits of New York and the traumas of Europe are behind them. F. Scott Fitzgerald has made his reputation with *The Great Gatsby* (1926) and has been trying to write *Tender Is the Night*; the heavy drinking that he had embarked on in his Princeton days—well before he met Zelda Sayre—has turned him into an ugly alcoholic. Zelda Fitzgerald has gone from being the beautiful young flapper-icon of the age to a mature woman who has grown beyond both the constant partying and the role, assigned her by Scott, of wife, mother, muse, and raw material for his fiction. She has tried to create her own, separate identity through artistic expression, first through writing short stories (which Scott signed with both their names or, sometimes, with his alone), then through ballet (which became an obsession), and finally through painting. However, the stress has precipitated serious instability and breakdown, which doctors labelled schizophrenia, and by 1933 Zelda has been treated in several institutions. When *Angel's Trumpet* opens, she has been out of the Henry Phipps Psychiatric Clinic of Johns Hopkins Medical School in Baltimore for several months; her novel *Save Me the Waltz* (1932) has been published, over the angry protests of her husband and only after he made cuts and changes to her manuscript; she is fighting to preserve some room and creative space of her own within the house and regime that Scott pays for and controls. He, however, feels he is losing control and arranges for an interview to take place at La Paix during which he will make Zelda understand certain facts in the presence of her doctor and a secretary, who will record the entire event.[7]

That such an *event* actually took place is striking enough. That the transcript has survived and been quoted at length by biographers is crucial. In choosing this dramatic crisis in the real lives of the Fitzgeralds, Pollock has unerringly selected *the moment* that will allow her to explore issues which have interested her at least since *Doc* (indeed, aspects of the family tension recall *Blood Relations*): Can one articulate the truth of interpersonal conflict and can one lay blame? What is an artist and what rights does he or she have over the lives of others? And what roles are open to women and how free are they to pursue their choices? Lurking behind these questions is

Pollock's long-standing quarrel with power, authority, systems, and institutions, which she warned us, as early as *Walsh*, force conformity, *normalcy*, and compromise on an individual. In the single, unbroken act of *Angel's Trumpet*, Pollock has stripped away all possible diversions, all possible outlets for emotional release, to focus tightly, economically on the life and death struggle between Zelda and Scott. At stake is nothing less than art and sanity – his art and her sanity. He *will* have control, the final say, authority over Zelda and her doctors, because he is the artist and he pays the bills; she and her doctor *will* comply. By the end of the play, Scott has won.

Or has he? If we go back to the historical record, we will remember that Fitzgerald died of alcoholism and heart failure in Hollywood in 1940. After *Tender Is the Night* (1934), which uses Zelda's life as its material and precipitated her relapse, he did not complete another major work (see Kendall Taylor, 284). In American letters he had been overshadowed by his nemesis Hemingway; on the international stage he would be eclipsed by greater writers like James Joyce, Malcolm Lowry, and William Faulkner. In real life Zelda was recommitted to the Phipps not long after the La Paix afternoon, and she died in Highland Hospital of Nervous Diseases in Asheville, North Carolina on 11 March 1948, when a fire broke out and she was unable to escape because the doors and windows were locked. With the vision of the mad—or is it the clarity of Cassandra?—Pollock's Zelda will *see* Scott's rather mundane collapse and her own fiery death in the final moments of *Angel's Trumpet*. She will also watch as the pages of the transcript created from those excoriating hours at La Paix drift to the floor, where they come to rest on a pair of red slippers. In Zelda's actual death only one slipper—its colour not noted by biographers—signifies because her charred remains could only be identified from dental work and a slipper found under the remains. In the play, however, the transcript and a pair of red slippers serve as tangible, readable indicators of what happened on that May day in 1933, and together with the play's title they point to some disturbing truths, including the possibility that Scott Fitzgerald did not ultimately win. After all, the transcript exists and it damns him; he did not achieve the fame he craved; the success he did achieve was inseparable from her life, which he cannibalized. And, finally, a contemporary Canadian artist he cannot control has taken the record and made us see it anew.

According to the Fitzgeralds' most recent biographer, Kendall Taylor, "whatever was amiss in Zelda's brain worsened that Sunday afternoon in May of 1933 when… Scott made it clear… that… he had the primary right to use their joint life as material for his fiction," and Taylor insists that "Zelda's story remains relevant to today's women who face similar challenges."[8] The challenge Pollock takes up is how to make art out of the ruin of these peoples' lives, and how to make that art meaning-ful. Inevitably, each reader and spectator will find his or her own meanings here, and these will range from a warning about being an artist to a declaration, rather like Shipman's at the end of *Moving Pictures*, to *never* relinquish your right to survive, to be true to yourself. But there is a deeply troubling undercurrent to this play that only a fine performance will dare to tackle, and it is this: if one person's talent conflicts in some way with another's, does that person have a right to survive, even at the cost— to sanity, freedom, or life—of the other? And if the struggle to survive involves a married couple, does the man's greater access to the powers-that-be necessarily legitimise his survival? On the stage, in this play, these questions come down to the actors playing Scott and Zelda. Zelda must be tragic all right, but also gifted, tenacious, funny, and more than a mere victim; Scott must be desperate, selfish, cruel, vindictive, and weak, but also an ambitious writer who *might* be famous if he can control and exploit Zelda's creativity. The role of Scott is not a sympathetic one; he is a combination of Peter Grimes and Pinkerton. But if Ben Heppner can perform Grimes and Placido Domingo give us Pinkerton, then an accomplished actor can *do* Scott.

———•———•———

At the end of *Angel's Trumpet*, just before the lights "fade to black," the transcript pages "slowly rain from Zelda's hands down onto the red slippers." Zelda does not pick up the slippers; she does not put them on or dance. But she does get the last words, those precious raw materials over which she and Scott have fought, and with them she describes her vision of a dance of death: "in the light and wind of the flames. I see the stockings dance!" The battle to become an artist, whatever the cost, has been joined, if not by Zelda Fitzgerald then by the artist who has dared to resurrect her and, in the process, make theatre and meaning from her life. In an interview with Martin Morrow for the *Globe and Mail*, Pollock explained that "after you've been in this business for a while, there can be a lot of self-doubt" and that she was attracted to stories like the Fitzgeralds' because they expose the "crisis of faith that you have about what it is you're doing" and whether you "are creating theatre that makes a difference" (R7).

Hopefully the production of *Angel's Trumpet* reassured Pollock that her art does make a difference. Certainly, the publication of these three compelling plays will demonstrate just how much of a difference can be made by excellent and demanding writing about things that matter. Here, as in all her work, Sharon Pollock creates characters that live on the page and the stage because the problems they face are perennial, fundamental, and important. Moreover, she has a command of language, unsurpassed on the Canadian stage, that equals the best English-language playwriting in the world. And last but not least, she is a superb story-teller. Her Nell Shipman is as unstoppable as Scheherazade; her Janet Smith refuses to die before having her say; her Zelda gets the last, the final, the visionary, creative words. All three are fighting off death and all three project their stories beyond the end of the play as they invite us to keep the story going.

These three plays confirm Pollock's stature. They demonstrate her commitment to serious theatre in which important social, ethical, and psychological questions are raised and to theatre where innovation or experimentation with structure and form are embraced. In them she probes more deeply than before into the roots of human motivation—ambition, survival, independence, creativity—and it is on this last subject, creativity, that she gives us new themes, characters, and challenge. Of course, she is on home ground with such an issue, but she does not limit creativity to the role of professional artist. In Pollock's world we are all potential story-tellers and we all have a responsibility to ourselves and to the collective story of our common humanity. In the final analysis, however, the ultimate test of a play's meaning and contribution is in production. With Pollock we have a major artist writing for the stage, and hers is a voice that needs to be heard. We need Pollock's plays to warn us about how much we could lose to domestic and public tyrants, to remind us of past mistakes, and to inspire us *never* to give up the struggle to create, like Eddie in *Fair Liberty's Call*, a better world. But to never give up requires a leap of faith and an act of the imagination. Put on those red shoes Pollock dares us. Put on the red shoes and dance.

———•———•———

1   *The Red Shoes*, with Pressburger's original screenplay, continues to fascinate movie lovers. The DVD includes archival stills, readings by Jeremy Irons, interviews, commentary, and memorabilia. *Ballet of the Dolls*, premiered in June 2002 at the Ritz Theatre in Minneapolis and, billed as the "latest 'Red Shoes'" revival "laced with more style," put its punk star in spike-heel, red shoes, no ballet dancer would touch. Powell's and Pressburger's cast included Moira Shearer as the artist torn between her ballet master and her composer husband, Anton Walbrook as the sinister, but magnetic Boris Lermontov, who plans to build the reputation of his company on the success of his young star, and Marius Goring as Julian Craster, the ambitious young composer who will marry Victoria but insist she give up her art to become his muse. Sir John Barbirolli conducts the London Philharmonic for the ballet performance within the film, which is a *tour de force* as well as an allegory of the frame narrative.

2   For primary and secondary bibliography up to 2000, see Nothof, 183-90.

3   See Pollock's comments in Nothof, 173-74. For a discussion of the play and the autobiography, see Grace.

4   Starkins' book is the best of the factual studies, but Lee approaches the question from inside the Chinese-Canadian community and, thus, contributes an important perspective to the story. Schlemmer's play, while interesting in production when it premiered at Vancouver's Waterfront Theatre in 1996, is incoherent and superficial as a text; we are seldom invited to go beyond the surface of the whodunit genre and the play provides an answer: Janet Smith was raped and murdered by the drunken son of a local politician. For a scholarly treatment of the socio-political context and ramifications of the Janet Smith case, see Kerwin.

5   Doris tells Andersen's fairytale. Pollock changes some of the facts: for example, the F.L. Bakers become Robert and Doris Clarke-Evans; Doris becomes a working-class English girl with a boozy mum; and Janet, who brings her own race and class prejudices with her from England, has had an affair with Clarke-Evans *before* her arrival in Canada. These, and other small shifts, provide Pollock with essential latitude to explore, not just one woman's dilemma, but the mores of an entire society at a given point in time.

6   In addition to serious plays by Williams and Pollock, Zelda has become the subject of a British musical: "Zelda—The Musical," by Roger Cook and Les Reed, is scheduled to open in 2003. For other works inspired by one or both of the Fitzgeralds, see Luce and Schaefer.

7   Pollock makes some significant changes to the historical record for her version of what happened at La Paix. Zelda's psychiatrist from the Phipps was Dr. Thomas Rennie, and it was Rennie, not Scott, who arranged the La Paix session. It was Dr. Mildred Squires who encouraged Zelda with the manuscript of *Save Me the Waltz* because she believed writing would help Zelda; the book is dedicated to Squires. Fitzgerald was livid; Squires was removed from Zelda's case. The stenographer was Isabel Owens, an associate of Fitzgerald's, and she used a dictaphone from which she later prepared the 114-page transcript. For details of this terrible afternoon, see Kendall Taylor, 274-76.

8   See Kendall Taylor, 371 and xix. Among the biographies, Taylor's is the most comprehensive and factually accurate. In some ways Mellow's is the more sympathetic to Zelda's plight, if in a slightly paternalistic way, and Milford's, which Pollock read, is the least satisfying because Milford tries so hard not to draw conclusions or make assessments. Each biographer quotes from the La Paix transcript.

————•————•————

Sherrill Grace teaches English at the University of British Columbia, where she holds the Brenda and David McLean Chair in Canadian Studies, 2003-05. She has published widely on Canadian literature, culture, and the arts, including drama, and is writing a biography of Sharon Pollock. Her most recent books are *Canada and the Idea of North* (2002) and *Performing National Identities: International Perspectives on Contemporary Canadian Theatre* (2003), co-edited with Albert-Reiner Glaap.

WORKS CITED

——•——•——

Andersen, Hans Christian. *The Red Shoes*. Trans. by Anthea Bell and Illus. by Chihiro Iwasaki. London: Neugebauer, 1983.

Cook, Roger and Les Reed. "Zelda—The Musical." Unpublished script, 2003.

Creery, Cybèle. "Where Dreams End and Begin." *The Calgary Straight* 16-23 March 2000. 8.

Fitzgerald, F. Scott. *The Great Gatsby*. 1926. Harmondsworth: Penguin, 1968.

——. *Tender Is the Night*. New York: Scribner's, 1934.

Fitzgerald, Zelda. *Save Me the Waltz*. 1932. Carbondale: Southern Illinois UP, 1967.

Grace, Sherrill. "Creating the Girl from God's Country: From Nell Shipman to Sharon Pollock." *Canadian Literature* 172 (Spring 2002): 92-111.

Johnson, Myron. Choreographer. "Ballet of the Dolls." With music by Craig Harris. 2002. http://www.balletofthedolls.org/red_shoes.html

Jones, Frank. "Who Shot the Scottish Nightingale?" *Trail of Blood: A Canadian Murder Odyssey*. Toronto: McGraw-Hill Ryerson, 1981. 207-18.

Kerwin, Scott. "The Janet Smith Bill of 1924 and the Language of Race and Nation in British Columbia." *BC Studies* 121 (Spring 1999): 83-114.

Lee, Sky. *Disappearing Moon Café*. Vancouver: Douglas & McIntyre, 1990.

Luce, William. *The Last Flapper*. New York: Samuel French, 1990.

Mellow, James R. *Invented Lives: F. Scott and Zelda Fitzgerald*. Boston: Houghton Mifflin, 1984.

Milford, Nancy. *Zelda: A Biography*. New York: Harper & Row, 1970.

Morrow, Martin. "Examining the Toxic Flower." Interview with Sharon Pollock. *The Globe and Mail* 2 March 2001. R7.

——. "Who's Afraid of Zelda Fitzgerald?" *The Globe and Mail* 9 March 2001. R6.

Nothof, Anne. "Staging the Intersections of Time in Sharon Pollock's *Doc, Moving Pictures*, and *End Dream*." *Theatre Research in Canada* 22.2 (2001):[**pending**].

——. ed. *Sharon Pollock: Essays on Her Work*. Toronto: Guernica, 2000.

Pollock, Sharon. *Walsh*. Vancouver: Talonbooks, 1973.

——. *Doc*. Toronto: Playwrights Canada Press, 1984.

——. *The Komagata Maru Incident*. *Six Canadian Plays*. Ed Tony Hamill. Toronto: Playwrights Canada Press, 1992.

——. *Getting It Straight*. *Heroines: Three Plays*. Ed Joyce Doolittle. Red Deer, Alberta: Red Deer College Press, 1992.

——. *Saucy Jack*. Winnipeg: Blizzard, 1994

——. *Fair Liberty's Call*. 1995. Peterborough: Broadview Drama, 2002.

——. *Blood Relations and other Plays* [*One Tiger to a Hill, Generations, Whiskey Six Cadenza*]. 1981. Ed Anne Nothof. Edmonton: NeWest Press, 2002.

The Red Shoes. Powell, Michael and Emeric Pressburger. Screenplay by Emeric Pressburger. London: Archer Productions, 1948. DVD. Criterion Studios, 1999.

Schaefer. George. Dir. *The Last of the Belles*. 1974. Platinum Disc Studio. Timeless Video, 1999.

Schlemmer, Katherine, with Sandhano Schultze and Wayne Spechet. "Disposing of the Dead." Unpublished script, 1996.

Shipman, Nell. *The Silent Screen & My Talking Heart: An Autobiography*. Boise, Idaho: Boise State UP, 1987.

Starkins, Edward. *Who Killed Janet Smith?* Toronto: Macmillan, 1984.

Sullivan, Rosemary. *The Red Shoes: Margaret Atwood Starting Out*. Toronto: HarperFlamingo, 1998.

Taylor, Kate. "Firebrand playwright still sizzles." *The Gobe and Mail* 9 March 2000. R1, 5.

Taylor, Kendall. *Sometimes Madness Is Wisdom: Zelda and Scott Fitzgerald, A Marriage*. New York: Ballantyne, 2001.

Williams, Tennessee. *Clothes for a Summer Hotel: A Ghost Story*. 1980. New York: New Directions, 1983.

Moving Pictures

Playwright's Notes

Moving Pictures is a theatrical tracing of the life of Nell Shipman, who as an actress sang, danced and hammed her way across North America in the early 1900s. In silent films she was a hit, known as the girl from God's Country from the title of her most successful film, "Back to God's Country." She established an independent production company and made movies in which strong women played principal roles, and a holistic view of the natural environment, the animal kingdom, and humankind prevailed. But as movie-making shifted from art to industry, the precepts that guided Nell to success became threats to her life as well as her career. Her last film script, written under a pseudonym, was produced in 1934. Her death in 1972 went unnoticed.

Moving Pictures explores the meaning of story-telling in our lives, and the artist's addiction to creation whatever the cost.

Moving Pictures was first produced by Theatre Junction, Calgary, Alberta in February 1999, with the following company:

Helen	Shawna Burnett
Nell	Thea Gill
Shipman	Lory Wainburg
Man 1:	
Edison/Bert Van Tuyle/Sam Goldwyn	Tony Munch
Man 2:	
Carl Laemmle/Ernie Shipman/Barry	Joe Norman Shaw

Artistic Director: Mark Lawes
Directed by Brian Richmond
Set & Lighting Design by Terry Gunvordahl
Costume Design by Deneen McArthur
Props Design by Kate Lawes
Stage Managed by Crystal Fitzgerald

The playwright wishes to thank:
Silvership Productions for its original commission;
Guardian Spring Productions for its developmental assistance;
Alberta Playwrights' Network for it workshop services.

CHARACTERS

HELEN	Nell Shipman, an actress, early years.
NELL	Nell Shipman, director & producer, mid years.
SHIPMAN	Nell Shipman, towards the end of her life.
MAN #1	
Bert Van Tuyle	American born; independent movie director and producer; Nell's lover and creative partner.
Sam Goldwyn	Polish immigrant; founder of Goldwyn Pictures.
MAN #2	
Carl Laemmle	German immigrant, founder of Universal Studios.
Ernie Shipman	Canadian immigrant; theatre and movie entrepreneur; Nell's first husband.
THOMAS EDISON	An old but still powerful man, inventor of the medium in which Nell Shipman creates, and a voice of authority.
BARRY	The 8-year-old son of Nell and Ernie – never seen, all lines are voiceover.

MAN #1 and MAN #2, when not directly engaged in a scene with the women, are always present on stage and observing the action. While they may seem to play roles assigned by the women, real power is vested in them. They have an ultimate interest in maintaining that power, in blocking any challenge to it, and in preventing any loss of it. As the play progresses, their assuming of character becomes more overt. Wardrobe bits or hand props that identify them are merely suggestions and may be as a production concept dictates. It's important that such bits or props be minimal, easily integrated into the action, and not impede the flow of the play. The degree and specifics of interplay between MAN #1 and MAN #2 and/or between the women and EDISON is left to the discretion and imagination of the director and his/her creative team.

There are 3 Nell Shipmans in the Play: HELEN, the young vaudeville and stock actress; NELL, the successful film star, director, screenwriter and producer; and SHIPMAN, the elderly has-been. They confront each other in the reconstruction of a life dedicated to the creation of play on stage and on screen. In that play, and in the transforming of her life experience into fiction, the woman discovers meaning that the actual living of her life did not reveal to her.

NOTE ON PUNCTUATION

In the script a dash followed by square-bracketed dialogue indicates an interruption of the line; within the square bracket are the words that complete the line were the character not interrupted.

MOVING PICTURES
— — • — — • — —

Black. A light picks out SHIPMAN sitting in a chair behind a desk. Less visible is NELL who stands behind SHIPMAN, and HELEN who is holding a script and standing behind NELL. A hand gun lies on the desk. MAN #1 and MAN #2 are on the periphery observing. EDISON is isolated from the others. SHIPMAN is reading a letter which she places on the desk. A moment of emptiness, the void. NELL leans forward and whispers in SHIPMAN's ear.

NELL
Play.

SHIPMAN
Can't.

NELL
Come on plaaay.

SHIPMAN
Can't.

NELL
Can so. *(snaps her fingers, then the sound of the rhythmic click of film running through a projector)* Play!

Black and white film plays on the set and the bodies of the characters, which provide the "screen." Elusive images flicker and flash, a strobe-like effect, illuminating SHIPMAN, NELL and HELEN. All are looking out as if watching a film they see playing on a distant screen, as the film plays on them.

EDISON
(a victorious public statement describing his greatest achievement; savours the words as they grow in volume and power) The... illusion... of... continuous... movement... through persistence... of vision the... illusion of continuous movement... through... persistence of vision The Illusion of Continuous Movement *(the film freezes)* through Persistence of Vision!

Twilight fills the space. The frozen film image bleeds out. Silence. A small moment frozen in time. The image of the "three in one" breaks apart. HELEN in her Lady Teazle costume steps away a bit, looking down at a script and resumé in her hand. She's studying her lines. NELL continues to gaze out as if she were still seeing the film. Neither acknowledges SHIPMAN.

SHIPMAN
(considering the implications of the words as they apply to her – a personal intimate statement of her failure) The illusion of continuous... movement... through persistence of vision The illusion of... (pause) I... have nothing to say... I have nothing to– (She looks at NELL and an irritation grows at NELL's focus on something that is not accessible to SHIPMAN.) I said I have nothing to say! (no reaction from NELL) I'm talking to you!! (no response) Do you know what everyone hates?... They hate it when you do that.... I said they hate it when you do that! Nell!... Nell!... I said everyone hates it! When your eyes glaze over. When they know you're not paying one bit of attention to anything they're saying. They could be telling you they're dropping dead in a month... "I am dropping dead in a month!" ...They hate it! I hate it! And you've always done it! As long as I can remember!... I said I'm dropping dead in a month!! (NELL still deep in thought makes a small sound of assent or dissent; she's not listening.) Would it make any difference if I were? (pause) What are you thinking?... Are you thinking about dropping dead? No, not likely. You're writing, aren't you? Inside your head you're writing. After everything you are still writing! You're not listening! You're writing!

NELL
(still absent) No.

SHIPMAN
No what? No what!

NELL
(less absent) What?

SHIPMAN
Exactly.

NELL
What did you say?

SHIPMAN
I said no what!

NELL
And I said I don't know what you're talking about.

SHIPMAN
And I said "exactly." I said "you're not listening, you're writing!" And you said "no" and I said "no what!" I said "no what" meaning "go on" and you don't know what I'm talking about so you can't go on because you aren't listening and I said "Exactly!"

NELL
And I'm saying "What the hell are you talking about!"

SHIPMAN
Oh for Christ's sake. I just want to hear you say no I'm not writing. Inside my head I'm not writing!

NELL
Why would you want me to say that?

SHIPMAN
Because it would be such a bloody lie!

> *HELEN looks up from her script to SHIPMAN, then, as the banter between the two other women seems to have ended she returns to studying her lines. NELL has returned to her inner contemplation. SHIPMAN studies NELL. After a moment she speaks. She's not letting go of the rant she's on. NELL is listening with only half an ear.*

SHIPMAN
So what're you doing now – considering sub-text?

NELL
I'm making something up.

SHIPMAN
You're a lousy mother, make something of that.

NELL
I could.

SHIPMAN
So you're writing. Alright. Here's something. Are you listening?

NELL
Ah-huh.

SHIPMAN
I'm telling you something.

NELL
Ah-huh.

> *A pause. After a bit the silence penetrates NELL's consciousness. She looks at SHIPMAN. SHIPMAN says nothing.*

Well?… Have you told me yet?

SHIPMAN
You're not that old, you're not senile, have you been told something or not?

NELL
You told me *(She thinks for a moment.)* I'm a lousy mother. Was that it?

SHIPMAN
No that's not it! I said "telling" not "told." This is it. You – have an incurable disease. The tests have come back and the doctor said you wanted to know.

NELL
Is this how he said to tell me?

SHIPMAN
Let's say – he gave no specific directive. So. Make something of that.

NELL
Did he say how long?

SHIPMAN
No.

NELL
(She prepares to write, gets out paper. Pauses and looks at SHIPMAN.) Are you lying?

SHIPMAN
About the story line – or the time line?

NELL
Either.

SHIPMAN
Everything's fiction. Isn't that what you say? So. Do you think you could write a script about that?

NELL
About what?

SHIPMAN
About dying! Pay attention! Do you think you could write a script about dying!

NELL
If I've got the time. The question is–

SHIPMAN
Why bother.

NELL
That's not the question.

SHIPMAN
Who'd buy it, who would produce it?

NELL
I said that's not the question!

SHIPMAN
It would be for any rational person.

NELL
I don't think about that.

SHIPMAN
Liar. *(pause)* What were you thinking about before?

NELL
Before? The flickers. I was thinking about the flickers.

> *HELEN looks up from the script; she loves the flickers, as early movies were called. She watches and listens to NELL and SHIPMAN.*

Standing at the back of the vaudeville house watching the flickers.

SHIPMAN
That was years ago. Past. Gone. Not important any more, no use.

NELL
Says who?

SHIPMAN
Says me. *(pause)* Now what're you thinking?

NELL
Now?

SHIPMAN
Yes now! After receiving the news.

NELL
What news?

SHIPMAN
The news, the news, we're back to that now! The doctor, the tests, the dying, the dead!

NELL
The fictional news?

SHIPMAN
You say the fictional news. I say Now, as I sit here, essentially destitute in my little rent-free cottage, courtesy of affluent old friends, Now as I digest the meat of the message, Now as The End looms up there on the screen – what can you make of it?

NELL
What can you make of it?

SHIPMAN
Nothing.

NELL
Make something.

SHIPMAN
Can't.

NELL
Can so.

SHIPMAN
Can't.

NELL
You always could.

SHIPMAN
Nothing to say.

HELEN
So play.

SHIPMAN
"The End." How's that?

NELL
Noo. The beginning, the middle, the bits in between, then the end, make something of it! Go on!

HELEN
Do it! *(She offers her script to SHIPMAN who refuses to take it.)*

NELL
Oh for God's sake! Play!

> *NELL grabs a pair of glasses from the desk and shoves them on her face; snatches the script and resumé from HELEN's hands, and plays, has fun*

with, sending up Mr. Gilmore, a Chicago producer of a third rate national stock touring company. He sounds like a Mafia wiseguy or Brando's Godfather.

NELL

(as Mr. Gilmore) Next!

HELEN

Helen Barham, Mr. Gilmore, student at Frank Egan Drama School Seattle – Lady Teazle.

Wears a Lady Teazle costume made by her mother, not a bad seamstress. She never falters, and steps into the scene playing to an invisible Sir Peter. NELL as Mr. Gilmore feeds HELEN her cues. HELEN's performance is rather extravagant even for restoration comedy and done with a veddy English accent. It's not a bad performance from a 13-year-old, and reveals punk, nerve, talent and daring. If she doesn't get the part it's not because she didn't give it everything she's got.

As you please, Sir Peter, you may bear it or not, but I ought to have my own way in everything, and what's more I will too.

NELL

(as Mr. Gilmore) So da husband has no aut'ority?

HELEN

If you wanted authority over me you should have adopted me and not married me. I am sure you were old enough.

NELL

(as Mr. Gilmore) T'ou my life may be made unhappy by your temper, I'll not be ruined by your extravagance.

HELEN

Am I to blame because flowers are dear in cold weather? You should find fault with the climate and not with me. For my part I wish it were spring all the year round and that roses grew under one's feet!

NELL

(as Mr. Gilmore) Yuh forget where yuh was when I married yuh.

HELEN

Yes' twas most disagreeable or I should never have married you.

NELL

(as Mr. Gilmore) I have made yuh a woman of fashion, of fortune, of rank – in short I have made yuh my wife.

HELEN
There is but one thing more you can make me to add to the obligation and that is—

NELL
(as Mr. Gilmore) My widow I suppose?

HELEN
Why do you make yourself so disagreeable to me and thwart me in every little elegant expense?

NELL
(as Mr. Gilmore) Had yuh any of dose little "elegant expenses" when yuh married me?

HELEN
I should think you would like your wife thought a woman of taste.

NELL
(as Mr. Gilmore) Yuh had no taste when yuh married me.

HELEN
And after having married you I shall never pretend to taste again! And now, Sir Peter (with an elaborate curtsy, and a pretty exit out of the scene) goodbye to you!

NELL
(as Mr. Gilmore) Not bad.

HELEN
(the high of performance still sustains her) Did you really think so, Mr. Gilmore? I did my best.

NELL
(as Mr. Gilmore) Ah-huh

HELEN
(that high is fading) Although one can always do better.

NELL
(as Mr. Gilmore, searching for the info on the resumé, trying to goad SHIPMAN into a response, into playing) Address, ah-huh… Age Age… Age Age Age, Age Age Age Age—

SHIPMAN
Thirteen!

HELEN
But I'm tall for my age! And I've finished school. Seattle Grammar School, class of 1905, that was in the spring, and I am not interested in further education... *(faltering a bit with the strain of the "interview")* ...except – as it – pertains... to the stage. I intend to be – an actress.

NELL as Mr. Gilmore considers her in silence, sniffs, looks at the resumé and back at HELEN who speaks with greater strength and conviction, almost daring NELL or SHIPMAN to contradict her.

I intend to be an actress!

NELL
(as Mr. Gilmore) Dis your right age?

SHIPMAN
I said thirteen.

HELEN
Thirteen, Mr. Gilmore, I'm tall for my age.

NELL
(as Mr. Gilmore) I can see dat. What would da folks say?

HELEN
Weeelll – my Great Aunt Marion – she lives in Scotland – I'm not American you know, I hope that doesn't matter, it shouldn't matter, but I'm Canadian and my parents are British and my cousin you see, or maybe an aunt, I've never met her, married a D'Oyly Carte so my parents are used to that and my Great Aunt Marion, I mentioned her before, well she would send the money for my musical education in Leipzig she said "A proper goal" she called it so – so everyone is used to the idea because ever since the age of the, age of the – but I'm not interested in that I've – I've taken piano and dancing and singing of course and now I'm here at Mr. Egan's and... *(pause)* ...I don't think my family would mind.

NELL
(as Mr. Gilmore) We'll ask. *(removing the glasses)*

HELEN
That means?

A cue for SHIPMAN to contribute to the story, to join in the play.

NELL
Come on Shipman, give a little.

No response from SHIPMAN.

HELEN
I've got it! Isn't that right? I'm cast! I'm going on tour with Paul Gilmore's National Stock Company! Ta Dum!

SHIPMAN
(attempting to puncture HELEN's balloon) Third rate national stock.

NELL
(helping HELEN out of her costume) But you done good.

HELEN
I did, didn't I? I really did. I knew they'd never let me in to audition so I had to sneak in. *(to SHIPMAN)* Isn't that right? I just – snuck in! And now I'm playing the *ingenue* in Mr. Gilmore's production of – Ta dum! – *AT YALE!*

SHIPMAN
It was only a knock-off of the real hit.

HELEN
I know I know, but this is it, this is the beginning, why aren't you excited? It's alright to get excited you know, you miss a lot when you don't. Just say Hooray! real loud. Hooray!! Come on Nell, show her how. I think she's forgot.

NELL
(going to a gramophone and cranking it) She saves it for *chimeras*, none left for life.

HELEN
Come on Shipman, real loud, Hooray! *(HELEN who is now in her bloomers and chemise does a cartwheel.)* You did it! Come on.

> *The gramophone plays. HELEN sings and dances for SHIPMAN. HELEN is sending up an act from a children's singing & dancing troupe at the turn of the century: The Boston Lilliputians. She does so with much physical illustration and a silly child's voice, attempting to seduce SHIPMAN into playing.*

Please go 'way and let me sleep
Don't disturb my slumber deep
I would rather sleep than eat
For sleep to me is such a treat, treat, treat,
I never had a dream so nice
Thought I was in Paradise
Waking up makes me feel cheap
So please let me sleep!

You did it, Shipman, yes you did! Hooray! Come on, Nell, your cue! How about Universal Pictures and – Mr. Carl Laemmle! *(With a clap of her hands MAN #2 buttons up a double-breasted suit jacket and dons eyeglasses.)* Play!

SHIPMAN
You don't have to yell.

NELL
(to SHIPMAN) Well, this should interest you – it's all about Money!

HELEN
You're on Nell!

SHIPMAN
I said you don't have to yell!

NELL
I'm not!

HELEN
Cue!

CARL
Why does it seem like you are?

NELL
Because nothing makes me feel more like yelling than you telling me to stop yelling when I'm not yelling!

CARL
Maybe that's it.

NELL
I want my check, Carl. *(CARL makes a move.)* And don't even think about putting your hand on my ass.

CARL
It's a friendly gesture and it's a nice ass. If you were a man I'd offer a drink.

NELL
I could use a drink.

CARL
A little hand on ass – it's how business is done.

NELL
I said a drink would be nice.

CARL
No one else complains.

NELL

You put your hand on my ass, first I'm going to complain and second I'm going to shove– [this scenario]

CARL

Now I feel like you're yelling again.

NELL

Look Carl, my last picture made 300 per cent for investors, and no check for me yet, why is that? And now Bert's– [out raising money]

CARL

That would be Mr. Van Tuyle, Bert?

HELEN

(a whisper to SHIPMAN) I'd say so *(snaps her fingers, MAN #1 slips on an ascot)* wouldn't you?

NELL

Don't get cute.

CARL

Only asking – former company manager Bert?

HELEN

(to SHIPMAN) What would you say?

SHIPMAN

I'm not playing.

CARL

He says you walk on water.

HELEN

Tell her, Bert. *(She tosses a cane to BERT. He has no disability.)*

BERT

So I say where are you shooting this film? And Nell looks over at Ernie and she knocks back her drink, bangs the glass down on the table, and she says, she leans forward and says "God's Country Mr. Van Tuyle." I say ah-huh. She says "where elephants can walk on water, and so can I." I say ah-huh. Ernie says "cut the bullshit Nell! It's Lesser Slave Lake, middle of winter, so what do you say, Bert."

NELL

I said I want my money.

CARL

Be nice Nell.

NELL
I'm a hell of a lot nicer than you deserve and I'm asking what's going on?

CARL
So – as a friend, Nell – I tell you. *(He pours himself and NELL a drink.)* You did two stupid things.

NELL
Only two?

CARL
Please. Keep your mouth shut, drink your drink, and listen. Two, let's say three, things. Who the hell knows how many things. Right now we are talking three things. Number one stupid thing. Cost overruns. You get brilliant idea on set and you execute that idea. Schedule or no schedule, budget or no budget. Kern River shots, end of movie, fall into this category. Number two stupid thing. Original writer is one of your producing partners. So you adapt his dog story for film, you beef up the woman's role—your role—and the dog gets a walk-on.

NELL
Hardly.

CARL
An improvement, but you don't handle him well. You intimidate this writer who is also producer.

NELL
It's hard not to. The top of his head touches my chin.

CARL
Comic potential. Use it in something.

NELL
How about I walk on my knees?

CARL
Whatever.

NELL
Look, you know "Back To God's Country" was a technical and an artistic success. It was worth every penny. So to hell with your cost overruns! And I improved Curwood's story, you said so yourself. The dog did not get a walk-on. The dog was very important. I love that dog! So what if the writer's peeved and we went over budget. The movie made money and I want my take.

CARL
You will get it – when Ernie signs the check.

NELL
  I need you to ask him.

CARL
  Why don't you ask Ernie yourself?

NELL
  Ernie.

CARL
  Yes Ernie. You remember Ernie. Your other producing partner? The one raising
  the money? Disbursing the funds? Signing the checks? That producing partner.
  Ernie. Your husband, Ernie.

NELL
  Ex-husband.

CARL
  Soon to be ex-husband. Which brings us to stupid thing number three. Second
  producing partner happens to be your husband. It is not good idea Nell,
  technically or artistically, to sleep with company manager when producer
  signing the checks is husband. If you had thought about that, I am sure you
  could have figured it out.

NELL
  I made "Back To God's Country" a hit. I got incredible footage out of those
  animals with care and honey sticks, no electric prods or trip wires! And believe
  me it was no picnic. You knew Ron Bryant? He died of pneumonia on location
  for Christ's sake! This ass you're so fond of? It damn near froze off, and poor
  Bert froze his foot off!

CARL
  Totally off?

NELL
  He froze his foot!

CARL
  Fuck Bert.

NELL
  I did.

CARL
  I know. Don't fuck around, Nell. Write that on something. Refer to it often.

NELL
  I wonder how often you've preached marital monogamy to Ernie Shipman, the
  great Canadian cocksman, over the years he and I have been married.

CARL
Ernie is a friend.

NELL
Does that mean you just stood in line for seconds?

CARL
You've a funny way of getting me on side.

NELL
I am owed money! You're the distributor and a friend and you can get it for me!
I want it!

CARL
Ernie won't sign your check. End of discussion.

NELL
I! …he can't do that.

CARL
He can.

NELL
So he can. Alright. Yes. I accept that. I was stupid. You're right.

CARL
And now you do what with this Bert.

NELL
Make my next movie, that's what. A winner. Building on the success of the last
one, the one I'm not getting paid for.

CARL
Neeell…

NELL
Everyone wants to see The Girl from God's Country. I am The Girl from God's
Country! And this time I'm not tied to a writer whose nose hits my nipple, and
I'm working with a man I respect who's not boffing everything in skirts – no
offense to Ernie.

CARL
Ernie would not feel offended.

NELL
No he wouldn't.

CARL
I tell you Nell where it is you go wrong – it's the way you make movies, and the movies you make.

NELL
How can you say that?

CARL
The lips move, the words come out.

NELL
I make good movies. Successful movies. How many have I written to keep Ernie in poker games and tarts?

SHIPMAN
You married him.

NELL
I was eighteen he was thirty-five that's the story, and we're not talking Ernie, we're talking movies, my movies, how many have I written, directed and played in, you tell me, how many?

CARL
You're a good little actress, Nell.

NELL
A good little actress?

CARL
Sam Goldwyn offered you a Studio contract year or so ago, no?

SHIPMAN
That's right.

CARL
You should have taken it Nell. See your name up in lights.

NELL
My name is up in lights!

CARL
You could have been a Star. (CARL will exit the scene, but not leave the stage.)

SHIPMAN
Could have been a star?

CARL
None of this bullshit, Nell. You could've been a star!

NELL

(*yelling after him*) Can you see me in a slinky dress, blond cu.. Could have been a star?! (*to SHIPMAN*) I am a star!

BERT

She's got sparks coming out of her hair and ideas pouring out of her head, she's got an eye for film and story, and a kick-ass attitude and by God if you aren't willing and able to follow her out on the ice you better pack your bags and hightail it home. (*will exit the scene but not leave the stage*) She's a beautiful woman… I can't walk on water but she – she sure as hell… she sure as Hell…

HELEN

(*yelling after him*) I sure as hell can!

NELL

(*as Mr. Gilmore, bellowing from the shadows*) Who told me yuh was an actress?

HELEN

(*shielding her eyes from the stage lights, looking into the balcony*) I did, Mr. Gilmore?

NELL

(*as Mr. Gilmore*) What's dat on your face?

HELEN

Make-up Mr. Gilmore?

NELL

(*as Mr. Gilmore*) Speak up! Can't hear yuh!

HELEN

Make-up Mr. Gilmore!

NELL

(*as Mr. Gilmore*) Never hear yuh past da sixth row! (*pause*) What! (*pause*) What! (*pause*) I said what!

HELEN

I've – forgotten the line, Mr. Gilmore.

NELL

(*as Mr. Gilmore*) What da hell are yuh wearin'?

HELEN

My costume?

NELL

(*as Mr. Gilmore*) No no no!

ELEN
My mother made it, Mr. Gilmore, she– [thought it was appropriate]

NELL
(as Mr. Gilmore) Find somet'ing else!

SHIPMAN
Give the kid a break!

> *HELEN changes into her HELEN costume as SHIPMAN watches.*

HELEN
(not complaining, it was a glorious time for her) Provide my own wardrobe… pay my own way…. Cheapest hotels… *(struggling with her costume change)* Can't do it. A hand please? *(SHIPMAN, after a momentary hesitation, helps.)* Mattress this thin! *(half an inch between her fingers)* Remember? And the smell?

SHIPMAN
(anything but a glorious memory) Still prickles my nose.

HELEN
I never noticed after a while. The luxury of an upper berth! *(SHIPMAN is about to contradict her.)* I know! Most often the hardest seat in the day coach, but sometimes? Right?

> *No response. The luxury of an upper berth was a rare event in SHIPMAN's opinion.*

Laundry – mine and what I wear in the show? I wash it—and me—in a small metal basin – and it's always at the end of the iciest hall why is that?!

> *For HELEN even the eternal iciest was a magical occurrence.*

And I dream – do you know what I dreamt?

SHIPMAN
My name up in lights. *(A foolish dream in SHIPMAN's opinion.)*

HELEN
Wrong! Hot water and food! Got a good review by a name critic at the Hundred and Twenty-fifth St. Theatre!

SHIPMAN
Closest I ever got to Broadway.

HELEN
Wrote letters home and never told them a thing that was true! *(an exceptional and fantastic achievement)*

NELL
Missed them.

SHIPMAN
Not really.

NELL
Not true.

SHIPMAN
Play then. *(She'll force NELL to acknowledge true family history.)*

NELL
Mummy

HELEN
who could make something out of nothing, whether it was meals for a week out of just enough meat for Sunday

NELL
or a glorious dress for the dance recital and a sailor suit for my elocution bit

HELEN
both of them made from some lacy bits and a dress sent by an English cousin

SHIPMAN
along with the Remittance check for Daddy, Black Expatriate Sheep of the British tribe. Admit it.

HELEN
(to NELL) Don't listen to her! Mummy was "an English Lady."

SHIPMAN
A Tragedy if she forgot her gloves.

HELEN
(horrified) Oh I don't think she ever forgot her gloves, do you?

NELL
Never!

SHIPMAN
So how about when brother Maurice was at war and Daddy and the dogs–

NELL
Daddy's war effort! A plan to raise meat for the table!

SHIPMAN
You're avoiding.

HELEN
I was a *bona fide* movie star then, least I'm saying I was.

SHIPMAN
Admit it.

NELL
He bought two rabbits!

HELEN
and before we knew it

NELL
there were hundreds of rabbits out in the yard.

HELEN
He'd sit out there

NELL
by the rabbit hutch

HELEN
smoking, he'd smoke out there, what did he smoke?

SHIPMAN
Navy cut.

HELEN
Navy cut! That's what he smoked!

NELL
But finally

HELEN
finally he took

NELL
five rabbits down to the butcher, and Mummy served them up for dinner!

HELEN
But! A terrible hush fell over the table

NELL
Nobody spoke

HELEN
Nobody ate

NELL

And finally

HELEN

by some kind of uncommon unspoken consent

NELL

we all got up, carried the pot to the yard

HELEN

Daddy got out a shovel

NELL

And we gave them a proper burial!

SHIPMAN

The dogs, the three of them, Daddy and the dogs.

HELEN

Four of them counting Daddy.

SHIPMAN

Out for a walk and a sit on the bench and a good smoke of that Navy Cut. He was old then.

NELL

No.

SHIPMAN

No what? Go on?

NELL

No!

HELEN

So take it back! New Play. Play! He loved being silly and singing his songs what were the songs? Come on Nell!

NELL

Gilbert and Sullivan.

SHIPMAN

And?

NELL

And he'd sing and he'd whirl round!

SHIPMAN

Yes, in a dance with – what? Come on, alliteration, you love it, dance with – what, with Death?

HELEN

A nice story, come on!

SHIPMAN

A dance with what?

HELEN

A handkerchief on his head!

NELL

He never fit in so he left Somerset

HELEN

and the family pottery works

SHIPMAN

That's not the story I'm thinking of.

NELL

and settled for a remittance. Alright?!

SHIPMAN

The End?

NELL

Shut up.

HELEN

Music Nell. Music!

> *HELEN begins to hum softly "Three Little Maids." NELL gestures and the gramophone plays. HELEN places a handkerchief on her head and sings, lowering her voice and dancing, an imitation of her father with his English accent, doing his silly bit singing and dancing.*

Three little maids from school are we
Pert as a schoolgirl well can be

> *HELEN places a handkerchief on NELL's head and pulls NELL into her song and dance.*

SHIPMAN

Come on Nell, what's the story?

HELEN & NELL
> (*singing*) Filled to the brim with girlish glee
> Three little maids from school!

SHIPMAN
> Daddy out for a walk and

NELL
> No.

HELEN & NELL
> Everything is a source of fun
> Nobody's safe for we care for none

SHIPMAN
> Finish the story.

HELEN & NELL
> Life is a joke that's just begun
> Three little maids from school!

SHIPMAN
> You afraid?

NELL
> No!

HELEN
> From three little maids take one away–

SHIPMAN
> So finish the story!

NELL
> My story!

SHIPMAN
> The Daddy story?

NELL
> My way!

SHIPMAN
> I can hardly wait.

HELEN
> So stop fighting and tell it!

NELL
(as she helps MAN #2, formerly CARL, off with his jacket which he hooks casually over one shoulder) It's "Back To God's Country," Lesser Slave Lake. Where's the hat, he's got to have the hat. (HELEN throws a cocky red hat to NELL who passes it to MAN #2 who tilts it back on his head.) There. Ernie Shipman!

SHIPMAN
He needs to speak to you alone, Nell.

NELL
(to SHIPMAN) So we're alone, and we're speaking, alright?

HELEN
How the hell do the

ERNIE
How the hell do the boys keep the cameras going?

NELL
I know. Ron's got a cold. It's all in his chest.

ERNIE
So I hear.

NELL
Can't afford a work stoppage.

ERNIE
That wouldn't be good.

NELL
I suppose Bert reports all of this so it's old news.

ERNIE
I get reports. From Bert. About Bert. I keep in touch.

NELL
He's good at his job.

ERNIE
Something like that. So I hear.

NELL
Ah-huh. Sooo. We're alone, Ernie. Why're you here? It's not Maurice is it? Nothing's happened to Maurice?

SHIPMAN
Avoiding.

ERNIE

He's fine.

NELL

Bloody war.

SHIPMAN

It's Daddy.

NELL

(*to SHIPMAN*) Daddy is fine! (*to ERNIE*) I know he's drinking a little too much but that's... that's because he's alone, with Mummy gone and, me here. He's fine. He looks after the dogs and the dogs look after him.... When I get home... not so busy, I'll see about... I'll see about someone to stay with him, or... or something like that. That's what I'll do when I'm back. He'll be fine, he's just

ERNIE

Stop talking Nell.

NELL

You know that's what I do when I'm nervous. Tell me I've nothing to be nervous about! Brother Maurice is fine, Daddy is fine so, get on with it, what's this about?

ERNIE

No, he's not fine. But we thought—I thought—it would be better to wait a bit. Not interfere too much with the picture. I knew you wouldn't want that.

NELL

No.... No.... Nothing, should interfere with the picture. Daddy.... That's good of you Ernie.

SHIPMAN

Nothing should interfere with the picture.

NELL

It's good work! And I'll.... After this one I'll definitely be The Girl from God's Country. You'll see.

SHIPMAN

And Daddy?

ERNIE

Had a stroke. They think it was a stroke. He was walking the dogs. Sat down for a smoke and, some passerby got him home. Not really much they could do. He was an old man, Nell.

NELL

He was an old man.

ERNIE
  (*as he's leaving the scene*) And I thought it best if we just waited a bit till we told you. Get most of it in the can. I figured that would be what you'd want.

NELL
  That's right... I wouldn't want–

SHIPMAN
  He's right. It is what you want.

ERNIE
  The Colvins looked after the funeral, Forest Lawn, by your mum, so it's all taken care of, don't worry. (*He doesn't leave the stage.*)

SHIPMAN
  Worry? All that matters is the movie, isn't that right?

NELL
  Other things matter.

SHIPMAN
  Nothing matters, only the movie.

NELL
  Daddy matters! And Ron, and Ernie he matters!

SHIPMAN
  "The dogs will look after Daddy" – Was that supposed to be funny?

NELL
  No not funny.

SHIPMAN
  "When I'm not so busy I'll see about someone for Daddy" – when would that be? The not so busy part, when would that be in this story?

NELL
  I don't know.

SHIPMAN
  Sure you know, tell me when?

NELL
  I don't know.

SHIPMAN
  Never! That's when. Another movie. An opportunity not to be missed. This one will be different! I'm an actress! I'm a star! I'm The Girl from God's Country! Pick it up! Say something!

NELL
I loved Daddy!

SHIPMAN
You loved work more. I heard that was the story.

NELL
No.

SHIPMAN
And "Ernie he matters." Did you ever love Ernie?

NELL
Yes but–

SHIPMAN
You were an unemployed actress whose norm was third-rate national stock and Pantages vaudeville when you met Ernie Shipman! You fell in love with his blue eyes and blond curly hair, and the jokes he made, and the people he knew, and the deals he cut, and it didn't hurt that he ran a better Stock company than you'd ever played in before! With lots of leading roles for you! Isn't that how it went?

NELL
All wrong, that's not the way that it goes.

SHIPMAN
And Barry, what about Barry?

NELL
Barry?

SHIPMAN
Your son, Ernie's son, where've you parked him this time?

NELL
You can't remember.

The shadow of a child begins to grow on the floor of the stage.

SHIPMAN
Military academy isn't it? And how old would he be now? Let me see, seven I think, and how long has he been there? Since he was six, and he'll be there for a bit, on and off

NELL
Play something different!

SHIPMAN
tuition paid by those wonderful English relatives, the ones you make fun of, "that British tribe" whose nice little cheques saved your neck more than once.

NELL
I don't have to listen.

BARRY
(voiceover) I hate it when you do that! I said I hate it when you do that! I hate it! Mummy!

SHIPMAN
It's not Mummy, Barry, it's Nell. She says call her Nell.

BARRY
(voiceover) You're not paying one bit of attention to me. I could be telling you I'm dropping dead in a month. I'm dropping dead in a month Mummy! And you've always done it. As long as I can remember. Listen to me! Some things are important you know. What're you thinking? Are you thinking about me dropping dead? No not likely. Are you writing? Yes you're writing aren't you. Inside your head you're writing. You're not listening to me. You're writing.

NELL
(Her dialogue overlaps with BARRY's voiceover.) No

BARRY
(voiceover) No what!... No what!

NELL
What

BARRY
(voiceover) Exactly!

NELL
What did you say

BARRY
(voiceover) I said no, what!

NELL
I don't know what you're talking about

BARRY
(voiceover) And I said exactly. You're not listening to me, you're writing. You said no and I said no what. I said no what meaning go on, and you don't know what I'm talking about so you can't go on because you aren't listening and I said exactly!

NELL

I said I don't know– [what you're talking about]

BARRY

(*voiceover*) Pay attention to me! I just want to hear you say no I'm not writing! Inside my head I am not writing! Say it!

NELL

Why would I want to say that?

BARRY

(*voiceover*) Because it would be a great big lie! (*pause*)

SHIPMAN

True?

NELL

Not like that, no, you're twisting the story.

The shadow of the child starts to fade away.

BARRY

(*voiceover, distant*) Mummy! Mummy!

SHIPMAN

Bert then. "Tell me, Miss Shipman, how is Mr. Van Tuyle?" Or is that just the Daddy story inside out?

NELL

I loved Daddy! If I'd known in time I'd have–

SHIPMAN

What?

NELL

I'd have gone to him yes I would!

SHIPMAN

"She leaves the picture to go to her father."

NELL

Maybe she would. I don't know if she would.

SHIPMAN

I do.

NELL

You're old. She never grows old.

SHIPMAN
You will.

NELL
She never grows old like you.

SHIPMAN
You will.

NELL
She never forgets the things that count.

SHIPMAN
What things would they be? Lay them out! Let's see! A list of her movies? The stories she's written? Is that what you mean?

HELEN
Stop!

NELL
I cried for Daddy. Not with Ernie. Not in front of the crew or the cast or the people milling around. I kept it inside. I said why wasn't I there, how could I leave him, what was I thinking. But – I thought I was doing something that mattered!

SHIPMAN
You thought recognition would come.

NELL
Now that you're old and no one remembers and you can't even remember you wonder if it was worth it! I know it was worth it!

SHIPMAN
Worth it. What is "it", what is it?

HELEN
Start over!

SHIPMAN
(to HELEN) What about Mummy? The real Mummy story? Title "How Mummy Died for Nell." Her movie, which one was it that time? You know she's spent her entire career peering through pine boughs, or swimming round waterfalls, or having a significant moment with a member of the animal kingdom. *(to NELL)* Don't you ever feel that?

NELL   You do. I don't.

SHIPMAN
(to HELEN) It was water that time. She was wet. Wet and cold. She'd been dunked more times than a doughnut and the take still wasn't right. She came down with the flu. *(to NELL)* When was it, 19 something or other? *(SHIPMAN knows the date.)*

NELL
You figure it out.

SHIPMAN
1918. *(to HELEN)* Yes, a bad flu. And Mummy tended poor Nell. Washed the flushed face, wet the dry lips, hovered over her like an angel. Looked after Barry. And poor Nell fell into a sleep. Like the princess no one could waken? A terrible sleep. Then do you know what happened? Once Mummy had made a pact with God. And she'd almost forgotten. God hadn't forgotten. *(to NELL)* She'd made a pact with God when you were ten days old on the night the doctor said you were dead. That night, she ran to the hill overlooking the bay with you in her arms. She held you tight in her arms, you, a little blue baby. She made a pact. And a light breath of wind off the water, hardly a wind, an ever so slight movement of air rose up from the water below and spiralled around her. And the dead baby started to cry. The night of the flu and your terrible sleep, she sat by your bed. When there was nothing more to be done, could be done, would be done, except wait for the sleep to take its terrible toll, Mummy remembered. Mummy went up and lay on her bed. She had made a pact. And in the morning, you woke up. She didn't. *(silence)* Play. *(no response)* Somebody. *(no response)* Play.

NELL
No.

SHIPMAN
(defeated) I win. *(silence)*

HELEN
(a whispered valiant attempt to start a new story) Daddy's voice was a tenor, and Mummy's, a very sweet alto... Nell? *(HELEN looks to NELL who doesn't respond.)*

EDISON
pin-point photographic images, spun to the accompaniment of a phonograph playing the sound track, resulting in a harmonious relationship with the moving pictures

HELEN
Play Nell.

NELL
(whispers) Can't.

SHIPMAN
Told you so.

EDISON
the motion of the subjects is documented simultaneously by three cameras – the subjects' movement is captured in bright relief

HELEN
(to NELL) Daddy lies on the sidewalk and Laddie stands over Daddy and won't let anyone near till they find someone who knows what to do. And the three dogs stay by his bed. Never leaving his bed. They look after him, Nell, like you said. Really, they do. That is the story.

EDISON
with a transparent, translucent film fed through the camera producing pictures of subjects in motion over an extended period of time

HELEN
(to SHIPMAN) This is the story! Ernie tells her and then she's alone. She goes to the place where they chain the dog from the movie. Two dogs really, Great Danes! Tresore for the vicious scenes because he is vicious and Rex for the gentle scenes because he is gentle, and the two of them looking like twins. She sits between them and she cries for Daddy. She cries, while Tresore and Rex each stretch to the end of their chains, put their heads in her lap and make small little comforting sounds. They love her.

EDISON
Persistence of Vision is the Central Illusion: the idea that isolated, fixed, and single images can appear to flow together, when brought successively into view, and intermittently advanced

HELEN
It's a love story, Shipman! Not old and not dying but living! National stock theatre on tour in Alaska? Exhilarating, Shipman! Going broke in Alaska? Stimulating, Shipman! Playing on pool tables shoved together for a stage? Galvanizing, Energizing – and bloody dangerous, Shipman! Why can't you remember?!

SHIPMAN
I remember.

HELEN
I know you remember. Boarding with an old lady and her forty canaries in Alaska? I never knew they shed feathers like snow in a blizzard. Educational Shipman, remember? Before movies and Ernie. Remember. That's when you fall in love. Really in love. In love for keeps. With the sky and the earth and the mountains.

SHIPMAN
: I did do that... I did.

HELEN
: You feel like a migrating bird flying home in Alaska.

SHIPMAN
: Not there yet, but close, getting close.

HELEN
: Charlie Taylor writes a play just for you, and what did he call it Nell? Nell?

SHIPMAN
: "The Girl From Alaska."

HELEN
: Everyone thinks you're the girl from Somewhere Away. From Not Where You're At. Isn't that funny? What does it mean?

EDISON
: There is a tendency to overheat if the picture passes too close to the light source.

HELEN
: I know what it means! Our last night in Alaska, I go for a walk with a husky. A big black silver-tipped dog. The Northern Lights are out, and I run with the dog, my feet pounding the ground with great shafts of light overhead. I run and I run with the dog. *I'm turning the earth with my running under a kaleidoscope sky.* That's what it means. We can play that Nell. Because that's how it was, and that's how it is, and that's how it always will be!

SHIPMAN
: Was it ever really like that?

EDISON
: *(fading although still audible)* This defect is not a major problem so long as the moving picture stays within certain parameters and distance from the source.

NELL
: Priest Lake?

HELEN
: We aren't playing that story.

SHIPMAN
: Not yet.

NELL
: But soon.

HELEN

Don't think of it.

NELL

Bert and the gun–

HELEN

Not yet! Try summer on stage in New York... try the toney Wall St. Cousins!... Try their painful teas for the poor relation, me!... Try... try Fun out with the Boys in the Chorus!

SHIPMAN

Fun. Till the leading lady pulls you aside, sits you down, and tells you all about "whoopsies" "muffhounds" "queers" and "other unnatural acts."

HELEN

"Do you want to be thought one of "them?" she says. She says "You will if you hang about with "them!" She says "Everyone'll think you're one of "them" – so ignore "them" she says – let "them" hang about with "themselves" – and she says "you hang about with... "Yourself!"

NELL

So I did.

HELEN

You didn't.

SHIPMAN

Well the end's the same. Alone.

HELEN

Get over it.

NELL

Did I cry?

HELEN

Of course you cried.

NELL

"She cried because they'd been her friends." That's how the story goes.

SHIPMAN

Does it?

HELEN

(to SHIPMAN) Would I lie? *(to NELL)* And you laughed. It was funny and sad. And you told the whole chorus what she'd said about "whoopsies!" and

"muffhounds" and you and the boys all laughed together and then you were sad and – Playing, keep playing!

SHIPMAN

Playing! For the Larger Lot in the Seats! For the Customers! For the Audience! For the Ones Paying the Shot!

HELEN

New York! *(does a little tap dance)* Got Fired! For? *(a "da da da da da dum!"* *hand off to NELL who doesn't pick up the cue; a second "da da da da da dum!" tap* *dance and hand off bit of business again)* For refusing to take a cut in pay when? Come on Nell – when?

NELL

(with no great enthusiasm) When audiences failed to appear.

SHIPMAN

So play for the Smaller Lot, for the Lot that you have to Pretend for, in order to Be In, in order to Get Out, in order to Learn, in order to Get Jobs, in order to Keep Jobs, in order to–

HELEN

Got a job with – come on Nell, with

NELL

With Jesse Lasky

HELEN

Jesse Lasky! Me playing the piano with five others on stage for – ta dum – *The* *Pianophiends!* *(as always, "performing" her story, and in the course of it* *managing to engage SHIPMAN and NELL more fully)* My piano downstage right. I could not get the piece of music ending the first act into my head and I couldn't use sheet music so – I fake it! Who could tell? Six pianos playing on stage? No one can tell! My fingers fly over the keys! They don't once touch the keys! Till a brush-up rehearsal when, as we approach the end of the act, and at a sign from Jesse's congenitally suspicious sister Blanche, everyone stops playing. But me. Who continues a beautifully mimed performance of this particular bit. As silence fills the air I gradually... bring... it... to... a... close.

NELL

How did I ever get hired?

HELEN

You know how! You played a bit of piano for Miss Lasky at the audition, and then, for Jesse, performed a highly effective crotch-splitting high-kicking bump and grind rendition of Alexander's Ragtime Band! *(the audition that seduced* *Lasky into hiring her; she sings while performing her "highly effective crotch-* *splitting high-kicking bump and grind rendition" of the first verse)* And did a reprise for my audition for Ernie Shipman!

Full orchestration comes in as HELEN continues her song and dance routine into the chorus of the song. ERNIE watches with a high degree of appreciation as she plays to him. He holds her resumé in his hand. The song and dance ends, and ERNIE redirects with difficulty his attention to reading the resumé.

During the following dialogue ERNIE studies HELEN's resumé with a bit of eye play between them as he does so. They are the focus of SHIPMAN and NELL who approach the couple.

SHIPMAN
In order to Find Love, in order to Keep Love, in order to

NELL
(to SHIPMAN) Alright. You were right. It was partly his hair. It was curly. He had blond curly hair. And he wore this funny little red hat that looked like a hunting cap and – didn't look like a hunting cap... I don't know what the hell it was, but on him it looked good. Made him look different. Not arty, or corporate or.... No bullshit. Ernie was not a bullshitter. Eyes... blue. A particular blue. Like a flower. Periwinkle blue. You don't see a blue like that very often. Little laugh lines. He was funny. It's hard to explain. He knew how to do things. How to get things done. He.... He just... I don't know, he just... I did love him. I did.

SHIPMAN
He was an asshole.

NELL
I don't know how I missed that.

SHIPMAN
A bullshitter.

NELL
I know. I know.... And he did get me jobs.... *(She is amused by, and kind of admires, ERNIE's blatant behaviour.)* Took all my money and spent it or lost it. Pregnant with Barry, I didn't have a thing for the baby. The morning after I delivered, the baby furniture and clothing and pram start arriving. All of this infant wear and apparel and.... He'd won it. While I gave birth, he played poker for all of these baby things. I don't know what we'd have done if he'd lost. I don't know what he'd put up for his ante.... Probably Barry! He would do that. He would bet the baby!

SHIPMAN
And his hair?

NELL
You know it wasn't that blond. A dirty blond. More of a sandy colour. Kind of dark. And he wasn't that tall, not really short... but

SHIPMAN
I know what you mean.

NELL
He was short. But I've got to stand by the eyes. They really were blue. This miraculous blue…. Sort of blue.

SHIPMAN
Muddy blue?

HELEN
(as she eyes ERNIE) Like a flower? Delphinium Blue?

SHIPMAN
Prairie slough Blue?

NELL
Leave me something. Come on.

ERNIE
(He's coming on to HELEN, she knows it and returns the ball, having fun.) Call me Ernie. I like the piece. You do it well. What else have you done?

HELEN
Two tours with national stock; *Pianophiends* with Mr. Lasky and his lovely sister Blanche.

ERNIE
(chuckles catching a subtle sub-text on "lovely sister") Bet there's a story there.

HELEN
You win.

ERNIE
I do.

HELEN
And a national and Alaska tour with Charlie Taylor; next with Sullivan and Considine in Seattle.

ERNIE
Playing what?

HELEN
Ingenues, Leading Ladies and Sads. It's on the resumé.

ERNIE
I like your voice, to hear you talk, go on.

HELEN
> Aahh, vaudeville, Pantages, Cora Mullaley and I have *The Apple Sisters Act*, we
> do a kind of parody of

ERNIE
> Heard it's funny. Maybe a little too smart but funny. How old are you? Hate to
> ask a lady but you look

HELEN
> Eighteen?

ERNIE
> What's your name again?

HELEN
> Helen Barham.

ERNIE
> Helen Barham. Sounds very – English.

HELEN
> It is English. So's Ernie Shipman.

ERNIE
> It's American – North American. Helen Barham. Sounds kind of – stuffy. You
> don't look like a stuffy kind of girl. Are you?

HELEN
> Am I what?

ERNIE
> Stuffy.

HELEN
> It depends.

ERNIE
> On what?

HELEN
> On what the role calls for.

ERNIE
> *(laughs)* You've got style. I like that… I manage a lot of people. They get work.
> They call me 10% Ernie because when I get you work, 10% is mine. Would you
> mind turning around? *(She does so.)* Looks good…. You're tall.

HELEN
> I'm just right.

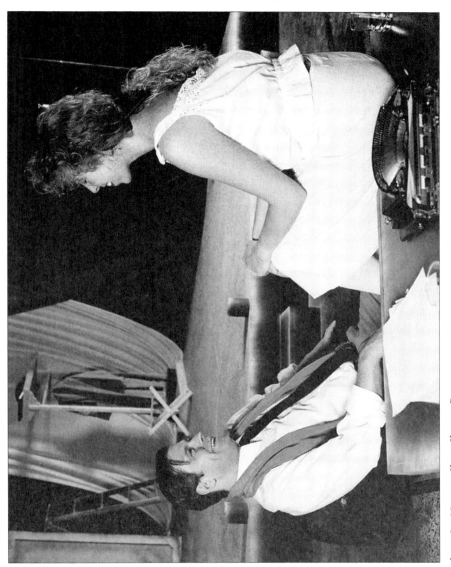

photo: Charles Hope Photography

l to r: Joe Norman Shaw, Shawna Burnett.

ERNIE
I like tall women. You've got something. It's partly the face. Something else. I dunno. I may be falling in love.

HELEN
I hear you do that on a fairly regular basis.

ERNIE
(laughs) I like you. You got something. How'd you like to play the lead in... *The Barrier?*

HELEN
Sounds good to me.

ERNIE
How does dinner sound? You see the order of things is important. If I'd asked you for dinner first you might've gotten the wrong idea.

HELEN
I still might.

ERNIE
(laughs) I like you.

> *During the following dialogue MAN #1 slips off his ascot, puts on a tie, clenches a dead cigar in his teeth and moves into the scene as SAM Goldwyn.*

SAM
Sam Goldwyn.

ERNIE
You're worth keeping an eye on.

> *The SAM/NELL scene, as it begins, interfaces with the ERNIE/HELEN scene as it ends.*

SAM
I been keepin' an eye on you. You done some good work for Vitagraph.

ERNIE
But we gotta do something about the name. How about Nell – Nell Wilson Nell Harris Nell Thompson Nell

SAM
Ernie had you churnin' out a lotta stuff for a lotta people

ERNIE
Shipman!

SAM
de Mille saw you on set at Vitagraph

ERNIE
It calls for discussion.

SAM
he mentioned your name

ERNIE
over dinner what do you say

SAM
Now you know we're contractin' some players and we're thinkin' of contractin' you.

ERNIE
Nell Shipman!

SAM
I got a contract right here. Seven years. Legal limit. You sign at the bottom.

NELL
Don't you think I should read it?

SAM
Never said don't read it. Always read the contract. Ernie teach you that?

NELL
It's a little something I discovered myself.

SAM
Smart girl. Don't let it get in the way of the camera.

NELL
I'm not smart enough to know what that means.

SAM
Movies're about one thing. *He wants it. Is he gonna get it?* Now go ahead and read, and sign there at the bottom. You know we're in the business of makin' money and one of the things that makes money is Stars, so in the business of makin' money, we make Stars. We can make you a Star. A commodity that sells the commodity we make.

NELL
I don't think of it that way.

SAM

Why should you? Nothin' to do with you. The deal is you're gonna make a lotta money, and we're gonna make a lotta money. Hell, when this business started nobody realized there was money to be made. But once we started throwin' movin' pictures up on that screen—'stead of some little kinescope parlour one machine one person—everything changed. Mass Audience! And when Carl Laemmle invested some money into makin' Florence Lawrence a Star and the box office took off, the industry realized hey, you make Stars you sell pictures! For a start you sell pictures. Then you sell what she wears. You sell what she drives. You sell how she looks. You sell how she lives, what she drinks, where she goes and you sell it on screen and off! You sell what she thinks! You sell what she stands for! You got yourself a vehicle to sell any goddamn material or immaterial thing you want! You can change the face and mind of America. *(pause)* You signed that yet?

NELL

I've read it.

SAM

For you we're gonna create a whole new look.

NELL

My name?

SAM

The name suits you, I like it. But the hair, the clothes, kinda roles you been playin'

NELL

And what kind is that?

SAM

and the stuff that you write, I've seen it on screen

NELL

What about it?

SAM

the female role, the kinda role you been playin'? – have you signed that yet?

NELL

The terms seem onerous.

SAM

Omerous! – omerous? What the hell does that mean?

NELL

Well, this says I work any hours you want, I play any roles you want, I make any movies you want. You can rent me out to any company you want for any reason you want. I'm to live where you want, go where you want, do what you want, and if I have a problem with any of this, I'm out at a moment's notice! That's what "onerous" means.

SAM

And you make a lotta money.

NELL

You make a lot of money. I don't. At least not in this contract.

SAM

I thought Ernie was smarter than this.

NELL

Say, if you see Ernie here you got a big problem.

SAM

I thought he had a thoroughbred, turns out you don't have the legs for it. Bit of mud on the track and you're runnin' last.

NELL

I'm finished at Vitagraph. I'm going into independent production. So – how about congratulations, Sam?

SAM

(starting to leave) All the world needs, another independent producer.

NELL

Hold it! Here's another hot flash! *(SAM slowly, leisurely, undoes and removes his tie and any other "Sam" bits as he listens to her.)* I'm writing the screenplay and I'm playing the role. Guess what? Female lead: strong woman. Male lead: sick husband. She beats arctic weather and villains. Saves husband and self with the aid of a great vicious hound everyone's afraid of but her. The villains all *want it.* But none of them *get it.*

Here's your contract. *(MAN #1, formerly SAM, smiles at her, ignores the contract and moves out of the scene but not off stage. NELL calls after him as he leaves.)* Why don't you try changing the name at the top and see if you can buy someone else? I'm not for sale!

SHIPMAN

Bad tag line. It puts him off. *(takes the contract and looks at it)*

NELL

He's an ass! I wasn't sure that he'd get it.

HELEN

An important ass?

SHIPMAN
In any version we care to create.

NELL
(grabbing the contract from SHIPMAN and tearing it up) And stupid!

HELEN
Well we can make him stupid – but was he?

NELL
They're always the ones running things.

SHIPMAN
Dangerous supposition, even in fiction.

NELL
Alright!

SHIPMAN
And you know another thing that you do?

NELL
What is it now?

SHIPMAN
You dick around with time, and with place – And with people! It complicates things.

NELL
It clarifies things!

SHIPMAN
How?

NELL
Gets to the essence, you know, fresh insight when you rearrange life? when you

SHIPMAN
Critics would differ.

NELL
"Cri-tics would differ?"

HELEN
It's alright to differ.

NELL
(to SHIPMAN) First structure, then critics? What the hell has that got to do with the story? *(to HELEN)* Why am I even talking to her? *(to SHIPMAN)*

Maybe the real problem's content eh? *(to HELEN)* I bet that it's content. She –
does not know – her own life!

SHIPMAN

Not the way that you tell it!

NELL

Nor apparently the way that you lived it You gave me your so-called "fictional
news" remember? The End looming up there on the screen and you said make
something of that, and I'm trying!

SHIPMAN

Oh you're trying alright.

HELEN

She means she can see that you're trying.

NELL

So! We have toured with the Gilmores, we have married Ernie, we've made
movies, we've had Barry, we have lost Mummy and Daddy, we are The Girl from
God's Country, we have turned down Sam Goldwyn, we have produced with
Ernie, we have been screwed by Universal and we have screwed Bert! Does any
of this ring a bell?

SHIPMAN

I find it painful you know.

NELL

(to HELEN) She finds it painful – while I struggle on, trapped by the burden of
bad teeth, failing eyesight, clogged arteries, stomach problems with spicy food
and never remembering where I've left the keys, she finds it painful? Who is this
old woman? I can't believe that it's me!

SHIPMAN

So where are we now?

NELL

(to SHIPMAN) With Bert! Dumped Ernie! With Bert!

HELEN

"The Nell Shipman Finance Company" remember?

NELL

She remembers alright! Producer, Star, Vice-president, me!

SHIPMAN

Oh yes – all the accoutrements, right?

NELL

That's right. A new car. Drove by the showroom, I saw it and bought it.

SHIPMAN

And a big house, right?

NELL

Are you suggesting that I was overly concerned with the acquisition of material goods? Is that what you're saying? Yes, I had a big house, a new car, motion picture company, hordes of animals, great clothes! I admit it! Do you feel better now? *(to HELEN)* She has a thing for material goods. I never had a thing for material goods. If I did, I'd remember.

SHIPMAN

How can I have a thing for material goods when at this stage of my life I have no material goods?! And you want to know why I have no material goods? Because you had a thing for material goods!

NELL

(to SHIPMAN) Well get this. Brownie the bear from "Back To God's Country?" I let her ride in the rumble seat of the car. I do. She has totally destroyed the rumble seat of the car. Does that sound like a thing for material goods?

SHIPMAN

It sounds like wanton destruction of material goods and irresponsible care of a bear.

NELL

And I've got raccoons, chipmunks, a skunk and a squirrel, a desert rat called Ignatz, two wild cats, and Nikki a desert gray fox, Tex who's a malamute and Angelic Nikisia the panama deer!

SHIPMAN

Don't forget Barry the boy.

NELL

And never forget the housekeeper for Barry. Housekeeper for Barry! Give me a death sentence for that! And I've got a room, special room, my room, where I, I cut and I edit!

SHIPMAN

And Bert?

NELL

What about Bert?

SHIPMAN

You tell me what about Bert.

HELEN

How about something new?

NELL

"Something New." That's the title of a crazy marvellous picture! Him. And me. Bert. Nell. Driving a Maxwell through the Mojave! 120 degrees heat. Horses or mules can't even go where we went. And we film it all. Good Work and I'm not afraid to say that out loud. Good Work! Are you listening out there! Good Work! This is the beginning! Real beginning. I am going to make movies that'll make people laugh and cry, and think a little. What the hell is wrong with that story?

SHIPMAN

Incomplete.

NELL

What's complete?! You tell me, what's complete? Who wants complete? Do you want complete?! I have never wanted complete! And neither have you!

MAN #1 has slipped on his ascot and picked up the cane to become BERT. He has a slight limp, the after-effects of the foot frozen during the filming of "Back To God's Country."

BERT

You lost it, Nell.

NELL

I'm not cut out to stand up in front of a bunch of pigeons, and justify every penny spent.

BERT

It's over budget.

NELL

It's not over budget! It was under budgeted!

BERT

You and I understand that. The investors don't. And you've got to explain it in a way they can understand and support.

NELL

They're in too deep, they can't pull the plug now.

BERT

They need reassurance and they need it from you.

NELL

We've changed the title. It's "The Girl From God's Country," I like it.

photo: Charles Hope Photography

l to r: Thea Gill, Tony Munch.

BERT

It's not titles they're worried about!

NELL

Whose side are you on?

BERT

It's the overtime on the flight shots.

NELL

So we have miles of film. I'd love more miles. Up there in the blue, blue sky, and those World War One Jennies skipping across the clouds, and you've got it on film, Bert, it's all there. The planes, wing tip to wing tip. Joe standing up in his Jenny cranking the camera, and me standing up in my Jenny playing the heart out of Marion. You on the ground. No communication between us. Director. Cameraman. Actress. We're reading each other's minds. A tiny mistake from the pilots? End of movie. Real end of movie. We've got to be crazy but just look at the footage!

BERT

And it's the cost overruns on the Canyon sequence!

NELL

We're fighting weather and we've got to pack everything in!

BERT

The menagerie keeps growing!

NELL

The animals are an asset! And I resent having to defend them on financial grounds!

BERT

They're expensive, not only to buy, but to house, to feed, and to transport!

NELL

But you can't put a price tag on what they give back! It's special between me and them! No fear. No abuse to make them perform. It's pure and it's spiritual and it reads. It all comes out on the film! For God's sake you're the director, you've seen the rushes, you know that!

BERT

But we can't afford to piss off the Backers and you know that!

NELL

All right! *(pause)*

BERT

You can't walk out of Board meetings, luv.

NELL
I know.

BERT
Tonight was a do-zer.

NELL
I was tired! And talk, talk, talking doesn't put footage on film.

BERT
It's their game in the Board Room. You've got to play their game.

NELL
I'm an artist, not an accountant.

BERT
But if you can't make the movie–

NELL
But I do make movies, so do you!

BERT
If you can't make the movie – or nobody sees it! What are you then!?

NELL
What am I then? *(pause)* Well, Bert, I'm trying to think of an answer to that…. Zero! Zilch! Blank Page in the Script! Do not waste my time asking questions that don't have an answer, Bert! Don't do that!

    Pause.

SHIPMAN
If you can't make the movie. Or nobody sees it. What am I then?

NELL
(speaking to BERT who is still and does not acknowledge her) I tell him I love him. I tell him we will finish this movie. I tell him it will be a success. I tell him Believe.

SHIPMAN
He says he believes.

NELL
I believe. What's wrong with that?

MAN #1
(as he removes ascot and jacket, rolls up his shirt sleeves, drops his cane and anything that identifies him as BERT or SAM) Timing, Nell!

Fading in on tape, the background noise of a small gathering of major players, a conspiracy, with glasses of good scotch in a smoke-filled room. The background noise plays under the following dialogue.

MAN #2

(*similarly removing anything that identifies him as ERNIE or CARL*) Timing and
Time and the Major Players!

MAN #1

We make product! And makin' product is gettin' very expensive. Movies are
gettin' expensive.

MAN #2

Unregulated Competition!?

MAN #1

Financial risk.

MAN #2

Unacceptable!

MAN #1

Creation?

MAN #2

I say each of us produces only the kind of movie each of us produces best

MAN #1

given our stable of Stars and directors!

MAN #2

Standardization of Product – Makes sense for makin' cars, makes sense for us
too.

MAN #1

Chryslers make Chryslers, Fords make Fords

MAN #2

So You – Westerns, you – Costume Dramas, – you – Musicals, and Comedies
you!

MAN #1

Distribution?

MAN #2

We gotta control the means of distributin' product to the guys who exhibit.

MAN #1

Gotta control all distribution companies

MAN #2
Preference is own em!

MAN #1
Exhibition?

MAN #2
We gotta control the means of Showing our product

MAN #1
We're talkin' movie houses here.

MAN #2
Preference is own the theatres!

MAN #1
Or place em under contractual obligation to us.

MAN #2
Packagin' of Product?

MAN #1
Every movie we make won't be a hit.

MAN #2
Every movie we make won't have a Star.

MAN #1
Every movie we make with a Star won't be a hit

MAN #2
So we control

MAN #1
Control the mix of movies our theatres exhibit

MAN #2
Some good movies, some B movies, some bad movies – they want a Pickford or Chaplin

MAN #1
they gotta take a whole package which is gonna contain—let's face it—some dogs.

> *MAN #1 begins donning those items which identify him as BERT; similarly MAN #2 is donning those items which identify him as CARL.*

MAN #2
No takin' one film.

MAN #1
It's a package of a number of films or nothin'

MAN #1 and MAN #2 pause.

MAN #2
Independent Producers?

Pause.

MAN #1
If...

MAN #2
...they make a movie we like

MAN #1
if... it fits in the package

MAN #2
if we can make a deal for distribution

MAN #1
and exhibition that works

MAN #1 and MAN #2 resume "dressing."

MAN #2
for us

MAN #1
we pick up the rights!

MAN #2
No problem with independent producers. *(He addresses NELL.)* It can't run nine reels. *(He puts on the glasses, he's CARL.)*

NELL
What do you mean, can't? It just did. The premiere was a roaring success.

CARL
Rented theatre, invited audience, roses for the Star, lots of friends.

NELL
Does that make it any less real? Everyone loved it!

CARL
It's too long for the market. If you want Universal to distribute, cut it.

NELL
   I took a lot of care with the edit.

CARL
   You took as long to edit as you took to shoot it. Right?

NELL
   The length of the film is the length of the film.

CARL
   And went 100% over budget.

NELL
   Do you want to distribute this film or not?

CARL
   Nine reels, no distribution.

NELL
   Get that time thing out of your head!

CARL
   Nine reels does not fit the program.

NELL
   Do you like the movie?

CARL
   You cut the film to market requirements or–

NELL
   Or what?

CARL
   Or your investors will take it, re-edit, and offer for distribution themselves.

NELL
   This film is my film.

CARL
   Not true.

NELL
   I've got a contract! And clauses! One being no interference from them with the edit!

CARL
   Contracts are made to be broken, what the hell do you think lawyers live on?

NELL
It's my film!

CARL
It's product! They invested in product! The length of your product takes it out of the market! Shorten the product then you got market! We're talking value of investment dollars and their right to pay-back against what? What are you putting against their dollars, Nell? What the hell is there goes up against dollars?

NELL
If they cut it they'll ruin it.

CARL
Believe me no one will notice.

NELL
I'll notice.

CARL
Who are you? People see what they get. They don't know the difference.

NELL
If I ever thought that, I'd quit!

CARL
So do yourself a favour. I got to go.

NELL
I'll sue.

CARL
The investors are shaking, the lawyers are laughing. *(starting to exit the scene)*

NELL
I'll write every exhibitor! I'll tell them the film's been butchered! Don't show it!

CARL
(stops) That would be stupid thing number – what, Nell. I'd think about it.

NELL
You bet I will! Take out a full-page ad! Tell everyone! I won't let them do it! It's not gonna happen, you'll see!

HELEN
I'll tell it! I want to go back and this time I'll tell it.

SHIPMAN
Do you think you can change it?

NELL

With a little song and dance maybe?

HELEN

"Carl Laemmle scene, Distribution of "The Girl From God's Country," an Independent Production"

NELL

I know, I know! How about he says "nine reels Nell? A little long maybe?" and she says "no problem, I'll cut it"!!…

Or it goes like this! Carl says "an epic film I am proud to distribute Nell" and she smiles modestly accepting the compliment!!!…

I know! She says "I'm so ashamed of the marvelous reception given the premiere of my film that I can not offer it for distribution unless it is cut! I insist that the film be cut!!!" *(a little tap dance to)* Da da da da dah! Is that it? Do you think you can tell it like that? Do you?!

HELEN

I know what they did. They killed "The Girl From God's Country."

BERT

(to NELL) They can't cut a third of a film and keep it coherent!

HELEN

(to BERT who does not acknowledge HELEN; he's talking to NELL) She knows what they did! *(to NELL)* Fresh start Nell. Fresh start.

SHIPMAN

No.

BERT

Do you think you were right about running that ad?

HELEN

(to BERT) We had to! *(to SHIPMAN)* And we have to. *(to NELL)* Go on, tell him. Priest Lake.

BERT

I don't regret your running the ad. Do you?

HELEN

Pine trees and mountains. Tell him. With the angle of sun and the light on the trees – the landscape, it changes.

BERT

It's going to cause trouble but–

HELEN
It changes in colour. It tells different stories different times of the day, different times of the year. See? Fiction. Even in nature.

BERT
I don't regret it.

HELEN
We have to, Nell.

BERT
You know it could kill us.

HELEN
Everything big. Nothing small, Nell. Puts things in perspective.

SHIPMAN
Don't want to.

HELEN
Have to!

BERT
We're lucky we aren't blacklisted, that's – assuming we aren't.

SHIPMAN
She's afraid.

NELL
Not afraid.

BERT
What?

NELL
I said Coolin, a little place called Coolin. Go there by train, then by boat to the end of the Lake. Wilderness, nothing but wilderness.

BERT
Why the hell would we want to go there?

NELL
Sell everything, start over.

BERT
I said why?

NELL

Create a spiritual home for the kind of films we make! Not just for the next picture, but a long-term location! Have you read my scenario? Working title "The Grubstake"—

BERT

But Studio work—

NELL

In Spokane! Not LA. Keep the cost down. We'll move the animals, bears, wolves, wild cats, the whole lot of them. Transport em. Build a lodge on the water – Lionhead Lodge for Film Casts and Crew! A Home for the Animals! What do you think? (BERT is rubbing his foot.) What's wrong?

BERT

It's nothing. Sell everything, the house, the–?

NELL

Move to Priest Lake! Shoot "Grubstake" in Idaho! What do you think?

BERT

I dunno.

NELL

Come on Bert. "Lionhead Lodge for Film Casts and Crew" a spiritual home for our films!

BERT

Do you really think we could do it?

NELL

Remember making "The Girl From God's Country?" When I nearly drowned twice? When the plane pitched and I almost fell out of the sky? The time my foot slipped and I almost fell off a mountain? When my dress caught and I could have burnt to death in the fire? I was never afraid. Not once. I knew we could do it. It just took another take. And it was a good movie, Bert. The investors cut it and killed it but even then – there're moments still in it, wonderful moments! I'm not afraid, and yes, of course we can do it!

SHIPMAN

When you say that–

NELL

Say what?

SHIPMAN

Say you're never afraid? When you think you can do anything? You are a danger. That's something I know.

HELEN
A danger to who?

SHIPMAN
To herself. And to others.

HELEN
Why's that?

SHIPMAN
She's either a fool or a liar.

NELL
So which am I? Tell me.

SHIPMAN
A... maker of fiction? A liar.

HELEN
And which one are you?

SHIPMAN
Me?

HELEN
Yes you. The Fool? Or The Liar?

SHIPMAN
Ah.... Which one am I.

EDISON
(faintly) the illusion of continuous movement with the appearance of truth is achieved through a persistence of vision in which the image dwells on the eye.

NELL
Never show fear. It grows and it spreads. Let them do what they want. Keep the film rolling. If Dumka the wolf wants to chew on my hair, don't move. Don't move. Pretend a slow soft awakening. Low baby babble of sound. Always that sound. Open eyes. Brown eye sees yellow. All caught by glass eye in black box. Lock brown eye with yellow. Film rolling. Keep rolling. If Brownie the bear hugs a little too tight, no fear. No fear. Glass eye, black box, babble words, almost words, always words, hear the words babble words always words you know me you trust me, trust me and know me and trust, the glass eye, the black box, the film, and the story.

SHIPMAN
Trust?... Trust you?... And the story.... Trust in the Story, and Telling the Story?

BERT
How'd it go?

NELL
A disaster.

BERT
How could it be a disaster?

NELL
I don't know! I've never done a trade show before. Room full of distributors backed by the majors and a couple of poor independents like me. It was supposed to be you! You're the one knows the distribution game, not me! And I'm the one's supposed to sell "Grubstake?"

BERT
So... how... did... it... go?

NELL
How's your flu or your foot and whatever it is that's kept you in bed?

BERT
I feel– [like hell]

NELL
Actually I don't care. At this moment I really don't care.

BERT
You can't keep it a secret. How did it go?

NELL
They hated it! They sat there like lumps, smoking cigars and belching. They got up and filed out at the end like the funeral service was over and if they got away quick, duty having been done, they could escape the graveside ritual. That would have been me. I was the graveside ritual!

BERT
Help me up.

NELL
I had to cut and edit this film at night sneaking up and down fire exits to avoid actors we owe money to! We've spent everything to make this movie and build Lionhead Lodge! We've hocked everything we own to get to this Trade Show! We're running out of money for feed and we need three thousand more for winter feed, and they hate the movie! Not a word to me, not a word!

BERT
Help me up.

NELL
I will not help you up! Who the hell's helping me up?

BERT
It's alright, Nell. It'll be okay.

NELL
Are you crazy? It is not alright or okay. It's a bloody disaster. And the worst thing is, the very worst is… I don't think the movie is bad! That's what's so terrifying! I don't think it's bad. I think "Grubstake" is good! Goddamn it, it is good!… But no sale…. So now what do we do?

Sound of a phone ring.

SHIPMAN
Fred Warren, independent distributor, makes a bid for "Grubstake"

BERT
Take it

SHIPMAN
Projected gross five hundred thousand, but a 75-25 split in His favour

BERT
Take it.

SHIPMAN
No money up front.

BERT
For God's sake, take it!

NELL
Not a good deal!

BERT
No other offers!

NELL
It's worth a lot more!

SHIPMAN
You'll take it.

NELL
I won't!

SHIPMAN
You'll take it.

NELL
I will not take it! I won't! I–! *(pause)* I… *(to SHIPMAN)* But I…. Have…. To…
I have to. It's not a good deal but, I'll take it…. Maybe… I can raise some money
on the strength of the deal maybe… work a deal, shoot some two reelers till the
money comes in maybe sell… sell a coupla stories till, till… I can do it… I
know I can do it. *(to BERT)* We can do it. We'll take it, and we can do it. But
I–!… But I'm telling you Bert! I think "Grubstake" is good. I do! It's good. What
do you think? *(pause)* What do you think?…

I said I think "Grubstake" is good! What Do You Think?! *(no response)* For God's
sake, say something! Just say it! It was bad! It was good! It was–

Sound of phone.

CARL
(moving into the scene, speaking directly to NELL) I watched your film this
morning, really enjoyed it.

SHIPMAN
Did you.

CARL
Beautiful scenery. Fantastic shots with the animals. Got excitement, got a
neighbourly feel. Holiday fare. We like it.

SHIPMAN
Do you.

CARL
Universal thinks it will sell.

SHIPMAN
It'll sell.

CARL
Seventy-five thousand up front, 50-50 split, in your favour.

SHIPMAN
Can't do it.

CARL
It's a very good deal. *(pause)* So. We can talk more advance but the percentage
offer– [is solid]

SHIPMAN
I've signed with Fred Warren

Sound of phone ringing and continuing to ring.

NELL

I thought nobody liked it. Nobody said that they liked it.

CARL

Nell, Nell, Nell, no one ever says anything at a trade show. *(sound of a second phone ringing.)* Warren eh? Not a major player. *(As he speaks he is removing any items of dress or hand props that identify him as CARL.)* You know the bankruptcy rate for fellows like him? *(sound of third phone ringing)* Too bad. A good little movie.

SHIPMAN

I've already signed.

Sound of four phones ringing.

CARL

You should stick with the majors, Nell. *(He snaps his fingers and the ringing phones stop.)* Independent distribution will kill you. *(Silence. He moves to the periphery watching as MAN #2.)*

HELEN

Play…. It's alright. We can play!… *(She laughs.)* Remember, remember that time driving into Seattle!? And seeing the billboard "Back To God's Country?" And your face? How big was your face?

NELL

(It was a nightmarish enlargement, not a cheering thought.) It was huge.

SHIPMAN

It was frightening.

HELEN

"See Nell Shipman in 'Back To God's Country'!" Ta dum! Not a paltry "with Nell Shipman" plus names in a cast list. No sir. It said "She's The Girl from God's Country!" And you were! The Girl From God's Country!

SHIPMAN

See Nell Shipman in!

NELL

Whatever.

HELEN

Remember those forty canaries in Alaska? The din and the feathers? It was funny. And seeing your name and the ad for the play on the floor of the birdcage? Finding that very same page and the ad and your face replacing the Sears Roebuck catalogue for use in the outhouse. You laughed.

SHIPMAN
It was funny. *(SHIPMAN and NELL can't resist smiling.)*

HELEN
And behind Pantages Vaudeville House in Spokane? Who was it put the apple on top of his head? Who gave you the gun? It was loaded. And you just took twelve big paces, you turned and you fired!

NELL
I did. I just did it! I fired!

The three of them laugh.

SHIPMAN
You did, you fired. Ka-pow!

HELEN
One lucky shot! No takers for seconds! Who was it you called the Top Top Banana?

Pause as she realizes who that was, and what became of the top top banana; she has inadvertently brought up something that causes depression.

SHIPMAN
That was Bert.

NELL
Trusting.

SHIPMAN
Too trusting.

NELL
Followed precisely the advice he got for his foot the first time he froze it.

HELEN
Prolonged immersion of said foot in kerosene in a washtub accompanied by the smoking of many cigarettes and the simultaneous imbibing of much hard liquor.

NELL
Bad advice.

SHIPMAN
And suffered the consequences everafter.

HELEN

Ending up with a permanent log. A log at the end of his leg. A dead piece of wood. At the end of his leg this – thing. It never really unfreezes he says. When it's cold, it hurts he says. When he walks, foot hits the ground, and it hurts.

NELL

Loved actors.

SHIPMAN

Loved me.

NELL

He believed.

SHIPMAN

After breakfast, up from the table, "Let's make motion pictures, Nell, let's go!"

BERT

What the hell has this place got that no other place has?

NELL

Charm! Simplicity! Reflects the purity, the spirituality of the Big Places! This Big Place! Priest Lake, Idaho! The mountains, the forest, the water, the scale of it all!

BERT

Oh yes, the natural setting we have in abundance!

NELL

It is not a compromise! It's the essence! We want that. If we weren't here we'd have to come here!

BERT

Not unless we were crazy. Well? Go on!

NELL

Movement and plot, plot based on small human incident in a natural setting.

BERT

And when they ask where's the cleavage?

NELL

You say "It's a reprieve from human villainy and sexual exploits." Do you think you could say that! Would it hurt you to say that!

BERT

Translation no sex and no villain.

NELL
How many times do I have to say it! The only villain is the tumultuous nature of the natural world! It works for our characters, and against them! We place our characters in that world as part of that world!

BERT
What characters?

NELL
The characters in the scenarios! Would you read the scenarios. Read them!

BERT
We've no actors! We've no money for actors!

NELL
We've got Barry for the kid's role, we've got me, I'm an actor, we've got Lloyd, I can get a guy from the lumber camp and Belle from the–

BERT
It's pathetic.

NELL
Listen! The animals. The animals play a big role.

BERT
Better be one helluva big role is all I can say.

NELL
Do you think I enjoy begging for film stock? Do you think I revel in pleading for a small cheque from the British Tribe while we wait for the money from "Grubstake?" Do you think I relish mixing flour, cornmeal, bran, rye, and lake water, arms in a trough up to my elbows, for feed? Do you think I savour poaching whitefish for dog food? Well let me tell you I don't! Let me tell you I would like it to be otherwise. But I make movies! This is what I have to do to make movies! To make my kind of movies! *(The shadow of the child is growing on the stage.)* They are set here because this is their setting! Animals work with us! Work for food and for housing and for care and affection because that is the world in which my movies live! And I work with people who give me the best they can give! I won't have you taking potshots–

BARRY
(voiceover) Mummy!

NELL
Call me Nell!

BARRY
(voiceover) Why can't I call you mummy?

NELL
 I'm busy, Barry!

BARRY
 (voiceover) Mummy?

NELL
 (a strong vicious attack springing from her impotence in other areas of her life) You
 don't call Brownie bear do you! And you don't call Laddie dog, and you don't
 call Angelic Nikisia panama deer! You don't call King horse! and I don't want to
 be called mum or mummy or mother!

BARRY
 (voiceover) Okay.

NELL
 I'm!

BARRY
 (voiceover) Okay.

NELL
 I am your mother. That's What I am. But it's not Who I am. Call me Nell please
 call me Nell and I'll call you Barry, Okay?

BARRY
 (voiceover) Let's run away Nell. Let's pack a lunch and go. Let's run away and
 find happiness over the hill. Do you think we could do that, Nell?

SHIPMAN
 Pack a lunch and find happiness over the hill.... Do you think we could do that
 Nell?

 *Silence. Although HELEN feels unable to "sing" or "perform" at this moment,
 she tries to provide some image of affection, love, happiness. The shadow of the
 child fades away during her speech.*

HELEN
 Brownie the bear sings. She has five songs that she sings. The sweetest when
 Barry and you lie down on a bed of pine needles beside her; most blissful when
 she sucks her paw pads; the saddest when she sees you leave with the huskies.
 Brownie still sings. She still can sing.

 *Pause. SHIPMAN picks up a yellow telegram, looks at it, holds it out. NELL
 takes it, opens it.*

NELL
 Fred Warren's gone under. Bankrupt. "Grubstake" held as an asset by creditors.
 No money from "Grubstake."

HELEN
Winter Tales.

NELL
Not yet.

SHIPMAN
Stories of. Winter.

NELL
Soon winter soon. Not yet!... Five little dramas're finished. We're sure to get something for them. An advance. Some money. Some... some

SHIPMAN
Barry?

NELL
I'll send Barry to friends.

SHIPMAN
We'll need

NELL
Food. For Bert. The handyman Robson. And me. Winter kitchen supplies for us three. Then there's supplies for

HELEN
the animals. Brownie and the two other bears; Sweetie, the mule who's kept by the creek, the sled dogs, the great Danes and Laddie

SHIPMAN
the eagles, the coyotes, the wolves, the foxes, the deer and the elk

HELEN
the raccoon and skunk; Bobs and Babs the two wildcats, Coalie my mare and Bert's gelding King; there's Angelic Nikisia and–

NELL
Feed for the animals, three tons of carrots and apples, the hard biscuits I bake, we've still got some hay, there's the game Robson hunts if the snow isn't deep. Then there's.... There's...

SHIPMAN
Not enough.

Pause.

HELEN

Remember the flickers? Vaudeville and the flickers. I'd rush from back stage to stand in the house just to watch. Over and over. I'd stand there and watch. Eyes glued to the Flickers.

Pause.

SHIPMAN

So... we... can.... Play.... Play for money. Charge money for tickets at Bonners Ferry and Sandpoint, they're big enough towns, you'd get a crowd. Show your copy of "Grubstake." Strut your stuff. You're a star.

NELL

I'm a what?

HELEN

(sings) Buffalo gal won't you come out tonight
Come out tonight come out tonight

> *Lights dim. The three "perform" for the Bonner's Ferry and Sandpoint audiences as black and white film is projected. The images can't be made out but shadow and light play across their faces, bodies and the stage. They'll perform as music plays. Reaction and the odd rude catcall from MAN #1 and MAN #2 as the audience. Although the three women are unified, working together, the strobe-like effect of the flickers fragments their unified actions.*

HELEN, NELL & SHIPMAN

Buffalo gal won't you come out tonight
And dance by the light of the moon
Darktown strutters play this song
Play this song play this song– *(music stops)*

NELL

A politician? Why that's an animal that can sit on the fence and keep both ears to the ground!

> *Drum punctuation and the music plays.*

HELEN, NELL & SHIPMAN

Come on along come on along
Let me take you by the hand
Up to the man up to the man
Who's the leader of the band
And if you care to hear the Swanee River
Played in ragtime– *(music stops)*

SHIPMAN

What's a critic? Why that's a legless man who teaches running.

Drum punctuation and the music plays.

HELEN, NELL & SHIPMAN
Come on and hear come on and hear
Alexander's Ragtime band– *(music stops)*

HELEN
An associate producer? Well… that's the only person who'll associate with a producer.

Drum punctuation and the music plays.

HELEN, NELL & SHIPMAN
I never had a dream so nice
Thought I was in paradise
Waking up makes me feel cheap– *(music stops)*

> *The three play this one moment from HELEN's audition for Mr. Gilmore as one individual sharing the line, with simultaneous robotic duplication of movement.*

HELEN
Am I to blame be

NELL
cause flowers are dear

SHIPMAN
in cold weather

NELL
you should find

HELEN
fault with the cli

SHIPMAN
mate and not with

NELL
me for my part I

SHIPMAN
wish it was

HELEN
spring all year round and

l to r: Thea Gill, Shawna Burnett, Lory Wainburg.

photo: Charles Hope Photography

NELL
  that roses grew

HELEN
  under one's feet!

  Sound effects for a pratfall, then music plays.

HELEN, NELL & SHIPMAN
  Everything is a source of fun
  Nobody's safe for we care for none
  Life is a joke that's just begun

  Flickering and music abruptly stop.

BERT
  Nell! Nell!! *(He staggers, walking with difficulty, wrapping a blanket round his shoulders. The three women observe his struggles.)* Where are you. *(silence)* Where are you? Where've you gone!? *(silence)* I'm talkin' to you! *(silence)* I'm talkin' to someone! Where are you, where– *(He falls down, and tries to get up unsuccessfully.)* Answer me!... Robson, Robson are you here, where are you? Where's Nell? *(silence)* Robson!.... Get up... come on get up... get the foot... under you... foot under.... You... get up – can't... get up... Robson! *(silence)* Help me!... Nell!... Nell!... I'm here, Nell! *(He starts to cry.)* Help me. I need help, Nell!... Get up. It's cold. Somebody help me! Somebody! Nell! Where are you, Nell! Nell. Help me Nell! Nell!!!

NELL
  Where's Robson?

BERT
  Robson? Where is he? I called, no one came.

NELL
  Angelic Nikisia is dead.

BERT
  A blizzard came in. Twenty below Robson said.

NELL
  And Nikisia is dead! Was extra bedding put out?

BERT
  I've been calling for you. Where were you?

NELL
  Were they fed? Did anyone feed them? Or did you just sit here with the blanket around you and whine!?

BERT

I can't get up! My foot hurts and I can't get up! There's been a blizzard outside. Where were you when I called?

NELL

Think! At the Benefit at Bonner's Ferry and Sandpoint!

BERT

That isn't true, that's a lie.

NELL

Don't start.

BERT

There's a blizzard so how did you get here?

NELL

I walked! And yes, there is a blizzard out there! I've hiked from Coolin to here, over the Lake where it's frozen and by beach where it's not. Forty miles. If I hadn't made Reader Creek last night I'd be dead. By rights I ought to be dead!

BERT

I know. I know where he is. He took the gun. He went hunting. The snow stopped and the wind died, and *(BERT struggles to get up.)* Robson said I'll see if I can get us some meat. That's where he is. He went hunting, Nell. That's where he is.

NELL

And Nikisia is dead of the cold. And the others– *(NELL leans down to help him.)* I asked you before! Were they fed? Did you feed them? Was extra bedding put out?

BERT

(grabs her arm, a steel-like firm grip and quickly levers himself up) You should be dead! Before you kill any more of us. You're killing us. Crazy ideas. You're crazy. Who said you were an actress? Who said it? I never said it! You couldn't direct. No. No, I could direct! You couldn't direct. I direct. What do you write? You write garbage and trash. You write little scenarios. Little – little notes. Little pieces of paper, not real writing. Little pieces of paper and I – I – I take them and I try – I try to make that garbage into story on film. Moving! Moving! Pictures! Pictures! Pictorial! Action! That Moves! That's what I do. I do it! This place is killing me. You are killing me. You're killing me. I won't let you kill me. No, no I won't. That's what it is. Killing me, kill you. Kill you, I'll kill you!

He shoves her away from him. Without touching her, a mimed realistic violent attack. He hits her in the stomach, backhands her across the face, grabs her round the throat, punches her in the face knocking her down. His frenzied attack is carried out in isolation from NELL although she reacts physically and audibly as if she were hit. She does not fall down. The sound of his laboured

breathing and exertions and her audible reaction are enhanced subtly on tape.
Physically exhausted, BERT stops. Inertia permeates the ambience of the space.
Silence.

SHIPMAN
He goes to the cookhouse. She walks down to the creek. She walks out on the
ice. She walks close to where water streams into the lake, and she stands on the
ice. A low sound, not a rumble. A clean sound, not a snap. She stands there. She
waits. Laddie comes. Laddie sits on her feet.

HELEN picks up the hand gun.

NELL
I remember it's time.

SHIPMAN
Time.

NELL
Time to feed Brownie and the others. Extra bedding. I – Robson helps. No
success with his hunt.

HELEN
I feed King the gelding the last of the hay. I tie my kerchief round his head and
his eyes. I shoot him for meat for the huskies. I take Bert into Coolin by sled
with the dogs.

HELEN replaces the gun on the desk.

SHIPMAN
He says it was the pain. It was because of the pain.

NELL
End result of the foot frozen how long ago? Now, blood poisoning, and threat of
gangrene, and amputation of toes.

SHIPMAN
He'll be back when it's over.

HELEN
Why?

SHIPMAN
He Believes.

NELL
Do you believe that?

SHIPMAN
He... won't be away... long.

HELEN
Still winter still winter still winter still

NELL
Film. Keep shooting film!

SHIPMAN
I mire Coalie the mare on a trail. We shoot her at dawn. There's meat for the dogs.

HELEN
The two wildcats go mad, chew each other to death.

SHIPMAN
The eagle turns on its mate. Tresore the Great Dane is poisoned.

HELEN
Who poisoned the dog?

NELL
The mule packing cameras stops in her tracks. She sways as she stands there in the snow. Robson will build a fire under her belly. Even this will not move her. Sweetie refuses to move. When Venus appears in the sky. Robson will shoot her.

HELEN
Carry on. This is the story.

> *HELEN goes to the phonograph and winds it as dialogue continues.*

NELL
I write. Little things.

SHIPMAN
He's better. Bert's better.

NELL
For *The Saturday Evening Post*.

SHIPMAN
Don't you think that he's better?

> *NELL looks at SHIPMAN. The phonograph starts to play a dreamy piece of music. BERT watches the three women. He is very slowly, carefully, casually, stalking them. He sees the gun, casually picks it up, carries it in an absent-minded way. The women appear quiescent, almost languid, as they search an internal landscape for details of this story.*

NELL
The Atlantic Monthly, sell a series of pieces.

HELEN
Spring. Spring comes. Spring always comes.

NELL
Feed and care for the animals, Laddie always close on my heels.

HELEN
And spring always comes?

NELL
Wait for the mail. A shipment of film. A magazine cheque.

SHIPMAN
Some word of success?

HELEN
Plans. New story, tell a new story. *(She starts to sway to the music.)*

NELL
A feature. Working title "The Purple Trail." Scenario. A woman– *(She falters before continuing strongly.)* A Strong Woman.

EDISON
Take, for example, a song on a phonograph record. Cut away seventy-five per cent of the record, and what remains would, of course, give the tune, but would it produce the desired illusion of hearing the song?

> *HELEN dances slowly. She's playing for herself. There is a falseness, a sadness, in her attempt to recreate fun. BERT's focus will centre on her.*

HELEN
So the two of us are in a spotlight downstage and it's a long piece of dialogue in which he's telling me off. Now he's a very spitty actor, my poor face is getting drenched and this spitty spray can be seen by the house because of the light. So – I take out one of those miniature Japanese umbrellas and open it, holding it up in front of my face. The audience breaks up and Gilmore fines me ten bucks, 50% of my salary!

> *She laughs, but it's forced and fades away. She continues dancing for several moments before attempting another story.*

By the end... by the end there's... there's six horses on stage along with six piles of you know what which I think they must have been saving all day for their moment on stage. So I get shot and I die. There I am, whirling round in my death throes, head tilted sideways like a bird, eyes squinty shut, trying to locate a spot where I can fall down and expire without landing in a pile of manure!

Many's the night I took a curtain call picking road apples out of my hair! *(The music quickens a bit, HELEN dances, and begins again.)* At the flickers, at the vaudeville house watching the flickers I'd stand–

> *BERT grabs her, holding her tightly. He doesn't seem angry, very conversational at first. HELEN doesn't struggle; his grip is painful. She stays very still, as do NELL and SHIPMAN the way one does with an animal that might attack if one makes the wrong move. Show no fear.*

BERT
> *(to the audience)* Glamour. They all said she had glamour. *(He smiles, perhaps even a small chuckle.)* Not the usual kind. Not that kind. Special. Her own kind of glamour. Do you think she's glamorous?… Do you think she's lovely?… Do you think you could love her?… I love her…. Yes, I do. I love her. I. Love. Her. Do you think you could love her?… Look at her. Look really closely! Look close! *(He grabs HELEN's face, pushing her face forward so the audience can examine it.)* Look at her!… I said look! Can you see her?… I love her…. Glamorous. Glamorous screen star! Does that look glamorous to you? Does it? Destroys everything. Everything. Lose everything everything lost. Everything lost everything gone! *(He shoves, throws, her towards the audience.)* Take her! Go on take her! I don't want her, you take her! You take her!!

> *He turns on NELL, who is isolated from SHIPMAN; he aims the gun at her.*

EDISON
Isolated snapshots selected from all three strips of film and reassembled afterwards achieve the most detailed representation.

SHIPMAN
The End.

HELEN
(getting up) Never Ends.

SHIPMAN
New story?

BERT
Don't leave me.

> *Pause. NELL and BERT lock eyes as he continues to point the gun at her.*

HELEN
Play.

BERT
Please…. Nell!

> *BERT puts the gun to his own head. NELL makes no move to stop him.*

SHIPMAN
In order to–

NELL
(to BERT) Go on!

After a moment BERT lowers the gun, it hangs loosely from his hand. The sound and flare of flame as MAN #2 scratches a match, lights a cigar. MAN #1 drops the persona of BERT, turns and tosses the gun to MAN # 2 who catches it, puts it in his pocket. There is an ambiance of threat or danger as the women watch MAN #1 as he joins MAN #2. The two men are on the periphery in shadow. They remain, watching, barely silhouetted, as the cigar smoke drifts around them.

NELL
(to MAN #1 and MAN #2 in defiance) Play! *(NELL turns her gaze from the men to HELEN and SHIPMAN.)* In order – to go on.

SHIPMAN
The animals will be lost.

NELL
To the San Diego zoo.

HELEN
Better than starving.

NELL
The lease on the land at Priest Lake

SHIPMAN
Will be lost.

NELL
I'll finish "The Purple Trail."

HELEN
Hokey title.

SHIPMAN
No one will back it.

NELL
Idea for a novel

HELEN
It'll be published

NELL
Magazine pieces and novels

SHIPMAN
Will anyone read them?

NELL
Movies.

SHIPMAN
Will anyone see them? *(pause)*

NELL
Never stop. Never stop, never.

Light starts to change.

SHIPMAN
Why not?... why not, Nell Shipman?

HELEN
Why not?

NELL
No choice!

EDISON
There is a tendency to overheat as the picture passes too close to the light source.

SHIPMAN
But we know the devil sits on the doorstep.

HELEN
Yes! But he'll never get in.

SHIPMAN
Why not?

HELEN
Because stories are barring the door! So – plaaaay. *(She picks up the script she was studying at the beginning.)*

NELL
(smiles) No choice.

EDISON
This defect is not a major problem so long as the moving picture stays within certain parameters and distance from the source.

SHIPMAN
(looks at EDISON) No choice!

> *EDISON's light goes out. SHIPMAN picks up the letter she'd had in her hand at the beginning. She glances at it, passes it to NELL.*

SHIPMAN
The "fictional" news... *(She looks up at the lighting booth.)* Gooo – to Black. *(lights start to fade)*

NELL
(to unseen techie in booth) Never! *(lights bump back up)*

SHIPMAN
Would you give me one moment's peace? I'm an old woman you know. *You're* an old woman!

NELL
We're an old woman.

HELEN
Never!

NELL
Never?

> *HELEN and NELL look to SHIPMAN.*

SHIPMAN
Alright. You've got me. Never! So – Play !

> *A tinny music hall piano accompanies a silent black and white film as it plays on the set and the bodies of the characters, which provide the "screen." Elusive images flicker and flash illuminating SHIPMAN, NELL and HELEN looking out as if watching a film they see playing on a distant screen, as the film plays on them. The shadows/silhouettes of MAN #1 and MAN #2 remain. The sound and the flickering black and white film stop. Hot pools of light on the three women. A moment frozen in time. Blackout.*

> *The end.*

End Dream

PLAYWRIGHT'S NOTES

End Dream, set in 1924, plays out the haunting inner and outer world of Janet Smith, a young Scottish nanny recently employed by the Clarke-Evans', members of their city's social and political elite. Janet confronts a household beset by mysterious activities, secret assignations, and sadistic game playing. Perhaps, as her employers insist, such dealings exist only in Janet's mind. A potential friend, were she able to overcome prejudice, is the Chinese houseboy, Wong Foon Sing, but even he is unable to prevent the tragic result of Janet's search for answers.

HISTORICAL NOTE

On a hot July day in Vancouver, British Columbia, 1924, a young Scottish nanny was found dead in her employer's basement. Rumours circulated regarding her employer's possible involvement in the drug trade and the nanny's awareness of it. However, the racism of the era made inevitable the accusation of murder against a Chinese servant in the household. Perhaps not so predictable was his kidnapping, torture, and detention for six weeks by hooded men, members of the local constabulary, possibly acting on the orders of the province's Attorney General. The Chinese houseboy was eventually charged and acquitted. The question of murder or suicide remained unanswered.

End Dream was first produced by Theatre Junction, Calgary, Alberta, in March 2000, with the following company:

Doris	Laura Parken
Robert	Jarvis Hall
Janet	Daniela Vlaskalic
Wong Foon Sing	Jovanni Sy
Wong Sien	Anthony Chan

Artistic Director: Mark Lawes
Directed by Sharon Pollock
Set/Lighting/Props Designed by Terry Gunvordahl
Sound Designer/Composer: Bob Doble
Costumes Designed by Deneen McArthur
Stage Managed by Crystal Fitzgerald

The playwright wishes to thank:
Anthony Chan for his assistance with the Cantonese dialogue;
Members of the Cast and Production team for their insight and contribution;
The Harry B. Cohen Foundation of Calgary for its sponsorship of The Playwright Chair at Theatre Junction.

CHARACTERS

JANET SMITH	a young Scottish woman, a nursemaid
WONG FOON SING	a young Chinese man, a servant
DORIS CLARKE-EVANS	the wife of Robert
ROBERT CLARKE-EVANS	a member of Vancouver's social and political elite
WONG SIEN	an older Chinese man

PLACE

The home of Doris and Robert Clarke-Evans. The room appears large, an infinite space. It exudes a hint of surrealism. It is minimally furnished. In the centre of the room are two deep maroon wingback chairs and beside each a small side table with table lamp. Directly behind the two wingbacks, and facing upstage, are two identical wingback chairs, a mirror image of the first two (referred to as "mirror wingbacks"). There is a drinks side table or bar, which has a bowl of fruit on it, in addition to decanters, glasses, etc. The floor is highly glossed and reflective. Whatever defines the space or room, as in "walls" or "panels," may appear solid but is translucent. Characters may pass behind or between them and be seen in silhouette when so desired.

Around the room's periphery, in a sense intruding on or violating the space, are twelve straight-backed chairs covered in red dust cloths and tightly bound with heavy black cord. In the area of the chairs is a wooden crate draped with a light-coloured large sheet. Behind it is a wooden chair, with arms, covered by an identical light-coloured sheet. One may sit behind the crate as if it were a kind of desk. WONG SIEN often sits there, as does FOON SING on one occasion. Others don't.

TIME

A compression of time in the heat of summer, 1924.

NOTES

None of the characters exit off stage. When not directly involved in a scene, they are on the periphery of the space where they may sit on or stand amongst the bound and dust cloth-covered chairs, and observe the scene; or they may sit in the mirror wingback chairs, and listen to, and/or observe the scene when it comes into their line of vision. On occasion we may see them in silhouette eavesdropping or moving behind the translucent walls.

NOTE ON PUNCTUATION

Underlined dialogue indicates the character is speaking in Cantonese.

End Dream

—·——·——

Act One

Black. In the blackness the sound of a long low exhalation of a flute, followed by an extremely loud resonant sound accompanied by a blinding flash that diminishes to an increasingly smaller point of light in the darkness. There is the acrid smell of gunpowder.

As the flash is diminishing to a point of light, the faint sound of blood moving through chambers, through channels, and the barely audible drum of a heartbeat, is heard. This sound continues under the dialogue.

A voice speaks in Cantonese. The voice is low, but not a whisper. As the soft low voice pervades, permeates the space, the face of JANET Smith gradually grows visible, seemingly suspended in space in the light. She is upstage centre. The shadowy figure of FOON SING is seen downstage some distance from JANET, a suitcase near his feet.

FOON SING
<u>I did not want this. I do care for you. Do you have feelings for me?… Can you speak?… If you can speak, speak. I'm listening.</u>

Faint light grows on an open newspaper held by WONG SIEN in front of him, obscuring his face as he speaks. He is near the crate. The newspaper headline reads MURDER!

The sound of a young child crying creeps in under the following dialogue. The sound of the pumping heart and the passage of blood is still present.

As WONG SIEN speaks, faint light grows on the shadowy figures of DORIS in a dressing gown and ROBERT in suit, overcoat and hat. Their focus is on JANET as they sit facing upstage in the two mirror wingback chairs. Smoke drifts from ROBERT's cigarette. Light glints from a glass DORIS holds in her hand and from which she occasionally sips. They are mostly invisible except for the drifting smoke and the glinting of the glass.

WONG SIEN
(reading from the paper) Wong Foon Sing, Chinese houseboy, kidnapped from the Clarke-Evans home more than six weeks ago, has reappeared. He claims he has been held at an unknown location and systematically beaten by hooded men. After six weeks of this captivity he is blindfolded and thrown in a ditch near Richmond. When found by police, he is apprehended and charged with murder.

JANET
No!

DORIS
>She'll stop. A little comforting is all it takes. I don't think she's really awake. We call her Rosemary.

ROBERT
>An hysteric. Imagines things.

DORIS
>Rosemary for remembrance.

ROBERT
>My wife is high-strung, but this girl? I'd say mentally unstable.

>*The baby's cries are fading and soon stop altogether.*

DORIS
>There, you see. She's stopping now…. Yes, she's stopped. She was stopping and now she's stopped.

JANET
>Has she!

ROBERT
>A young woman away from home, running, no doubt, from problems there?

DORIS
>We'll never know.

ROBERT
>But I wouldn't take her word for things.

>*WONG SIEN lowers the newspaper. He looks at ROBERT and ROBERT goes to him.*

>Oh she may have said things, thought things, wrote things–

WONG SIEN
>A diary?

ROBERT
>It won't reflect reality. *(as he takes the newspaper from WONG SIEN)*

WONG SIEN
>Reality?

>*Light begins a slow invasion of the space.*

ROBERT
>I say it will not. *(as he crumples up the newspaper and discards it)* Reflect reality.

The focus of ROBERT, DORIS, WONG SIEN and FOON SING is on JANET who is isolated and some distance from them. They observe her impassively.

In the light we see her more clearly now; a young woman in coat and hat. The room is full of shadow. She looks as if she's been abandoned at the front door shortly after entering this house.

The almost subliminal ba-boom of heartbeat and the sound of moving blood are still present. The sound seems more a stirring of the air than an actual sound. One feels it as opposed to hearing it.

JANET slowly stretches out one hand towards ROBERT and WONG SIEN as if to ward off a blow or perhaps to confirm their presence.

The sound of wind chimes, as if someone had brushed up against them or as if stirred by a vigourous wind although we hear no wind. That sound takes JANET's attention from the two men. It breaks the moment. She is now unaware of any presence except her own in this space.

Noting that her outstretched hand is gloved she removes first one glove, then the other. She reaches down with one hand to pick up her suitcase. As she does so FOON SING picks up the suitcase at his feet. JANET is surprised her case is not on the floor beside her. She looks up and for the first time takes in the room as light begins to brighten in it.

After a moment's pause she steps forward, enters the room slowly. Once JANET passes DORIS' chair, DORIS gets up, her focus on JANET and moves to the periphery to observe her better. JANET is unaware of DORIS' passage. JANET scans the room, taking in its furnishings. The room seems unreal to her. She approaches the drinks table, tentatively stretches out her hand to touch its surface. When she touches it, that low rushing sound of blood moving through passages stops immediately but the soft sound of heartbeat continues with a growing lapse of time between each beat.

JANET relaxes; she runs her fingers along the surface of the table, then round the rim of a crystal glass, picks it up, turning it upside down to look at its base. She smiles at the thought of its expense, and puts it down. She's more at ease now. She picks up an apple from a bowl of fruit, gives it a small toss, and is about to bite into it when she's startled by a voice.

FOON SING
  I have it.

JANET steps back a few steps.

I have what you are looking for.

ROBERT, WONG SIEN and DORIS watch. They may sit on or stand among the red bound chairs. JANET and FOON SING are unaware of their presence.

JANET
(*pointing to the suitcase*) That's mine, I... mine, my suitcase. It belongs to me.

FOON SING
<u>Are you afraid?</u>

JANET
Don't. I don't.... Don't. Understand.

DORIS
Willie!

> *FOON SING looks at DORIS. A silent communication occurs between the two.*

Wil-lie?

> *FOON SING carries the suitcase to WONG SIEN and gives it to him somewhat formally. WONG SIEN acknowledges the receipt of it with an almost imperceptible nod of the head, places it by the crate, sits in the chair behind the crate and continues watching.*

> *Meanwhile DORIS drains her drink, places the glass on the drinks table and addresses JANET. As dialogue continues FOON SING approaches JANET and takes the apple from her. He wipes it and replaces it in the bowl and makes DORIS a fresh drink.*

DORIS
Willie. It's an odd name, don't you think? For him? But I'll tell you something. It's a private joke. His name? A private joke? A very silly private joke and you must promise not to breathe a word of it. Never never never! Not to a living soul. See? You're a member of the family already. Privy to private jokes and sworn to secrecy. Oh yes.

> *DORIS places her hands on JANET's shoulders. The sound of the low random ba-booms of heartbeat stops once DORIS touches JANET.*

DORIS
(*whispers*) Sworn to secrecy.

> *DORIS slips JANET's coat and hat off. JANET is wearing a blue apron-like overall over her dress, an unexpected discovery for JANET.*

We're informal. (*giving FOON SING the coat and hat, he gives her a drink, and stands by*)

And you'll find out all sorts of things. What Robert puts on his toast, who Robert – you remember Robert?... My husband Robert? Who hired you? That Robert, sight unseen by me? The hiring that is. He'd sent me on you see, he'd stayed behind. He took a chance, well he had to didn't he? But – never mind that! It's none of your business!… What were we talking about? Ah yes, "find out all sorts of things." You'll discover who it is I'm never at home to, why Rosemary cries in her sleep, how Robert manages to – Why does Rosemary cry in her sleep!? Discover that! And quickly too! And – and put an end to it. That would be heaven. No more crying babe in the night. Or afternoon. Or – whenever! It drives me mad. It does you know. *(noticing FOON SING)* Go! Go! Coat and hat now go!

As DORIS continues, FOON SING leaves the immediate space with the hat and coat and places them on one of the bound chairs. He will return, take a small sharp knife from his pocket and sit in a mirror wingback chair listening as he wipes and cleans the knife. Its blade catches the light occasionally. He may glance round the corner of the chair at JANET.

Sit. Please. Anywhere. What was I saying? *(She sits, JANET doesn't.)*

JANET
I don't–

DORIS
I know, I know. The joke. The private joke. Not so private really. We tell everyone. But! Secrecy. Se-cre-cy. A mark of loyalty. Robert's Big on Loyalty. Perhaps you know that. Do you know that?

JANET
I–

DORIS
Well it's a secret that everybody knows. Sooooo, nobody speaks of it. It's that kind of secret. It doesn't make sense does it? It's silly. It's this. The joke is the secret and the name is the joke. I don't think that's right. It may be the other way round. Which would make it… I don't know what. But. The houseboy's name is Wrong. Not wrong. Wong. Wrong and Wong. That's funny isn't it. No, perhaps not. But let me get this straight… Willie is wrong. That's not his name. His name is Wong. Wong Foon Sing. Now do you understand? It doesn't matter! Call him Willie! You sit down. I'll stand. *(She stands.)*

Wong Foon Sing. During the war – Sit down! *(JANET sits down.)*

During… the war… my husband Robert, that's *(doing a little dance step)* R-O-B-E-R-T! served in the RAF! *(She laughs.)* All initials you see? The RAF, officer, pilot, hero – Hero Hero, that's what I thought. Nursing then. Injections? Hooo! Ah! Forget that. So anyway he had two batboys over the course of the war, now what the hell's a batboy? I don't know. But anyway they were both called Willie. Willie you see? You understand now don't you? Easier to remember you see? The name. For Robert. Wong Foon Sing. I mean. Just call him Willie. Easier to remember. And it suits him Robert says. And he should know. Don't you agree?

JANET
I don't–

DORIS
And that's the joke! His name is Wong we call him Willie! Oh Robert tells it all so much better than I do. Actually – actually it's a stupid story. Not so much stupid as – Silly! It's not easier to remember! It's the same for God's sake, maybe less so, don't you think? God! Everything! The baby you know? Everything.

JANET
I don't–

DORIS
It's so bloody exhausting. It's all so…

A pause and silence as DORIS studies JANET.

DORIS
He did mention me didn't he? During the interview in London, he mentioned me?… You didn't think he was…. A widower did you?… Did you?… But how romantic…. If it were true how…. Romantic. Only – it's not. He's not. I'm not. And – you're not.

JANET
I should go.

DORIS
Why? Does the Asian menace concern you?

JANET
I beg your pardon?

DORIS
The houseboy. Wong Foon Sing. Willie whatever. Does his presence in the house concern you? Well for God's sake speak up. I desperately need someone for Rosemary and there's no way Willie can go so let's get that out of the way right now! Actually – there's no way you can go. Until you've repaid your passage over. That was the understanding wasn't it? If you leave within the year you'll have to repay the cost of your passage? Yes? Where did you meet him? Don't you remember? I met him in a hospital, he was, you know, and I was, and… and… of course that's neither here nor there! Although it led to… so… where?

JANET
What?

DORIS
Did – you – first – meet – him–?

JANET

Meet who?

DORIS

You're not very bright are you? Then again, Rosemary's only eight months old so I don't suppose it matters. Where did you meet him, my husband, met, where, him? God, I've been spending too much time with Willie. I think I'll sit down. *(She does so.)* I'm sorry. I really am. It's just that you've caught me at a bad time – between getting up and going to bed.... That's a joke. You can laugh. You know how to laugh don't you?

JANET

I don't think–

DORIS

Ahh yes, best not to... best – not to.... Oh I am... so tired...

> *DORIS studies her hands, tracing the veins in her right wrist with the index finger of her left hand. She cradles the wrist in her left hand and studies JANET who touches the blue overall apron she's wearing, feeling the texture of the cloth as if that would prompt a memory of it.*

You're a very pretty girl. Has anyone told you that? I'm telling you that. You – are a very – pretty – girl. Do you smoke?... Can you sing?...

> *JANET starts to get up. DORIS grasps JANET's hands drawing her back into the chair.*

DORIS

I used to be able to sing.... Can you sing? *(She gazes into JANET's eyes and sings slowly.)*
My bonnie lies over the ocean
My bonnie lies over the sea
My bonnie lies over the ocean
Oh bring back my bonnie to me
Bring back bring

> *JANET reluctantly joins her. ROBERT stands up.*

JANET & DORIS

Back oh
Bring back my bonnie to me to me
Bring back bring back

> *DORIS stops singing.*

JANET

    Oh bring back my bonnie to me
    My bonnie lies over the ocean
    My bonnie lies over

       She stops, DORIS motions for her to continue, and she does so. Light is
       changing.

JANET

    My bonnie lies over the sea
    My bonnie lies over the ocean
    Oh

       JANET sees ROBERT. She stands up, continues singing, joyous, more upbeat.

JANET

    Bring back my bonnie to me

       She runs to him, he picks her up swings her round as she sings. DORIS and
       FOON SING watch. WONG SIEN stands up.

JANET

    Last night as I lay on my pillow
    Last night as I lay on my bed
    Last night as I lay on my pillow
    I dreamt that my bonnie was dead
    Bring back bring back

       ROBERT puts her down, moves away from her, seeming to reject her. Faint
       fragments of "Lullaby and Goodnight" a cradlesong, played note by note on a
       piano is heard. JANET is aware of DORIS, FOON SING, ROBERT and
       WONG SIEN staring at her, and of her isolation from them. Her voice begins
       to falter.

JANET

    Oh… bring… back my…
    Bonnie to me to me
    Bring back bring… oh
    bring…… bonnie
    To… me…

       She stops. She speaks to FOON SING.

It hurts. My head… it hurts.

       She brings her hand up to feel her head just over her right eye. FOON SING
       moves to her, one hand on her shoulder, the other holds the small knife.

       The single notes of the piano continue, growing slightly distorted.

DORIS steals a glance at ROBERT, then kneels and slips her hand down between the cushion and the arm of a wingback chair. ROBERT looks at her.

JANET looks to FOON SING as if for an explanation of their actions. FOON SING holds the knife up to shush JANET.

A soft freeze as WONG SIEN approaches JANET and FOON SING. He studies them for a moment.

WONG SIEN
Wong Foon Sing testifies he is in the kitchen. He hears a loud noise. He believes it comes from the laundry room in the basement. *(takes the knife from FOON SING's hand and feels the blade)* Foon Sing enters the basement and finds the body. *(crossing to the periphery with the knife)* Blood is still flowing from the wound.

DORIS
(showing ROBERT a silver cigarette case she's retrieved from the chair) Cigarette?

ROBERT shifts his gaze from DORIS to the case. DORIS releases the spring, it pops open to reveal cigarettes.

ROBERT
No.

DORIS takes a cigarette out of the case. As she slowly closes it, the music and lights fade with the closing. She snaps it closed and we snap to black. The music ends abruptly with the snap out.

Immediately, a ka-chunk sound with light as FOON SING turns on a table lamp. A low hum fills the air. DORIS is no longer kneeling.

DORIS
She's put out, I can tell you that!

DORIS is in a soft freeze although she is speaking in an animated fashion. FOON SING, JANET and ROBERT are in one dimension of time and space, and DORIS in another. When DORIS finishes the following speech, ROBERT and JANET will end up in the same place as they were when DORIS began speaking. During her speech the following occurs.

FOON SING stands by as a good houseboy. He is still and watching.

JANET smiles at ROBERT, and sits on the arm of a wingback chair, crosses her legs, and slides her skirt up a bit showing her leg, ROBERT circles round her, perhaps running his hand down her cheek or touching her hair as he passes. JANET might attempt to take his hand for a moment but it slips away on her. Their flirtation ends as the speech ends.

She thinks you should have told her, you should have mentioned it in the notice. The London advertisement. The fact there was a Chinaman in the house. She thinks it's against the law. Someone—her mother, sister, brother—Someone has given her a copy of the Women and Child's Protection Act. She thinks it's against the law to employ a white woman when Chinese are employed and work in the same place. Well, we're hardly a restaurant or a laundry are we? So it doesn't apply. This is our home. Well – for the most part – our home. So piss on! – Piddle – on the Women and Child's Protection Act. I told her that. Not in so many words but I told her!

A ka-chunk sound, the hum stops, the light brightens, the "double dimension" has disappeared.

Willie get Robert's coat! – And a drink for him Willie, a drink!

FOON SING takes ROBERT's coat and hat.

ROBERT
It's alright Willie, I can get it myself.

FOON SING, after placing ROBERT's coat on a chair will join JANET, the two of them standing by, seemingly neutral servants at attention as they watch and listen.

DORIS
She wonders about the furniture.

ROBERT
Really?

DORIS
There's... so much of it.

ROBERT
What did she say?

DORIS
Nothing. But I knew. I sensed it. You met her, I suppose, just the once in London? At, the interview.

ROBERT
Mmmnn.

DORIS
And then, I suppose, another time? To let her know it had gone well?

ROBERT
Mmmnn.

DORIS
To offer her employment? Is that the way that it went?

JANET moves closer eavesdropping, ROBERT is aware of her approach.

ROBERT
Something like that, yes.

DORIS
She's a pretty girl.

ROBERT
Do you think so?

DORIS
And not too bright.

ROBERT
You think not?

DORIS
She's perfect.

ROBERT
Is she?

DORIS
For Rosemary.

ROBERT
Oh?

DORIS
For. Rosemary.

ROBERT
And don't "interfere," is that what you mean?

DORIS
You! – Are a Bastard!

DORIS delivers a strong slap to his face but before it lands ROBERT seizes her wrist. JANET makes a move closer and FOON SING speaks sharply to stop her.

FOON SING
Stop!

ROBERT holds DORIS' arm and wrist at an awkward angle. A breathy long low resonant note on a bamboo flute. The sound ebbs and flows in the air.

DORIS
You think I don't know what goes on? I know what goes on.

ROBERT
You should.

DORIS
You took advantage.

ROBERT
Or vice versa.

DORIS
Me, I took advantage of you? Bloody liar!

ROBERT
(*releasing her*) You're slipping in front of the help, luv.

DORIS
Who's slipping?

ROBERT
(*moving to the periphery, giving JANET a wink as he passes*) Lady Doris.

JANET laughs and turns watching him go. Still laughing she turns to look at DORIS.

DORIS
He – is slipping! That's who. Him!

JANET suppresses her laugh, After a moment of standoff between the two women, DORIS moves away to sit facing upstage in a mirror wingback chair. JANET laughs.

FOON SING
Can you hear that?

JANET listens to the flute. The sound dies away.

FOON SING
All is quiet now. Very peaceful. (*He begins to clear away the drink glasses, and stops by JANET.*) You.... You come long way.

JANET
Move.

FOON SING
Me – Foon Sing *(He smiles as if sharing a joke.)* Willie – come long way too.

JANET
Get away.

FOON SING
Foon Sing help.

JANET
Don't talk to me.

FOON SING
Not need my help?

JANET
No, no help. You have your place. I have mine. Stay – in your place.

FOON SING
Where is my place?

JANET
Kitchen, the kitchen.

FOON SING
And where your place?

JANET
Here. Anywhere here. *(whirling round and around ending up by the drinks table with the fruit bowl)* Anywhere I want to go. Now you go! *(She picks up an apple and bites into it.)*

FOON SING
If you like. *(starts to leave and stops)* While you here. In house. Foon Sing can help.

JANET
Go!

FOON SING
Friends, eh? *(leaves for the periphery)*

JANET
(starting after him) Not friends, no!

ROBERT
(interrupting her move) Doris tells me there's been a small misunderstanding.

JANET
Well I'd hardly call it small.

> *FOON SING turns back and stands by unobtrusively, the good servant, observing the scene.*

ROBERT
What would you call it?

JANET
I'd call it – well– (*She drapes herself in a wingback, eating the apple.*) to start – I'm not prepared for a Chinaman – sir. I never thought I'd be sharing the house with one. Alone in the place. When you're out, and when – "Mrs. Clarke-Evans" – is out. I thought there was a law.

ROBERT
Not for domestics, Janet, no I'm afraid not. (*takes her hand and strokes it*)

JANET
Well I thought there was.

ROBERT
But there isn't. And if there were such a law forbidding white and Oriental domestics in the same household what do you think would happen?

JANET
A girl like me would be safe.

ROBERT
A girl like you would be safe?

JANET
Yes.

ROBERT
The Oriental is very industrious Janet, and the white domestic, not you of course, but generally speaking the white domestic is not. (*He kisses the crook of her elbow.*) Industrious. So the results of such a law – I leave it to your imagination, mmn?

JANET
(*moving away from him*) None of it's like what you promised.

ROBERT
Unemployment would rise among white domestics. (*following her, putting his hands on her shoulder*)

JANET
And I'm a nursemaid, not a domestic! (*She shrugs him off.*)

ROBERT
But you get the point. There isn't a law.

JANET
Well I thought there was.

ROBERT
Well there isn't! (*He pours himself a drink.*) And if there were it would not bode well for the employment of white domestics, or – A Girl like You.

> Pause.

I'd hate to see you out on the street, Janet. Alone. And owing a large sum for your passage from Britain. I mean what could you do?

JANET
I could do anything.

ROBERT
Do you have any – references?

> Pause.

JANET
You're not like you seemed.

ROBERT
Aren't I? But then again, what is?

JANET
I thought that we–

ROBERT
(*lifting JANET's chin with his hand so she looks into his eyes*) Did Doris surprise you? I know I should have prepared you but I thought if you knew you might not come. And you know that I need you, eh? (*tracing her features lightly with his index finger, then kissing her lightly*)

> *The sound of a bang on a wooden door. FOON SING looks towards the periphery.*

ROBERT
That's a good girl. (*another bang*) Willie!... (*FOON SING approaches.*) This, Janet, is Willie, Wong Foon Sing, our houseboy, and this, Willie, is Miss Janet Smith, Rosemary's nursemaid. You may call her – Nursie.

> *The sound of two bangs on a wooden door as JANET reacts to "Nursie."*

(*smiling at her*) I'll get it.

He moves towards periphery and WONG SIEN.

FOON SING
(*offering his hand to shake*) Nursie.

JANET
(*slaps her apple into it*) Not my name, thank you very much.

FOON SING
Now Nursie your name. Yes? Nursie. Willie. (*relaxing into a wingback, begins to eat the apple*)

JANET
No! Never Nursie name! My name, my name is Janet Smith!

The sound of a faint clickety-click and low resonant rumble of a train.

JANET
Miss! Janet Smith! Miss Smith to you, Willie! And don't you have something to do?

The sound of a sharp train whistle, increasing change in the lighting. During the following a faint clickety-click and low resonant rumble increase in speed and volume as the speech does in intensity and volume. Her words are the tip of her thoughts. Her mind is moving too fast for her tongue to keep up. She grows increasingly distraught. FOON SING observes her anguish, as do the others who may draw a bit nearer to watch her.

JANET
Something,
To do!...
I can do anything! I could!
I should go...
I could go! How could I go?
No! Not!
Well I could...
Find!... Away! the
The money the money is good
Too good! Good and
he's he's he's a good looking man
Well! Off!
Off I did it again acted on something I felt I never thought...
I never do. Think! Think I think too much!
Like. My. Dad. Says. He says...
Right he's always right!
No no he's not he's not right old bugger he's not right good to be rid of him yes yes I feel too much that's right I feel too much no, not that I, feel, not –
I do I feel I–!

Suddenly she sees something, a strange reflection from the floor.

Sometimes!
Just on the edge!
Corner of my eye!
Something!

She gets down on the floor trying to see into it.

Klimmer!
Klimpse!
Kli–!

She sees herself reflected in the floor, but it's a horrific image of her with a terrible head wound. She has to scream to be heard above the sound of the train.

Dream
that my bonnie
is dead!!

All sound abruptly stops. Silence. She touches one hand to the wound in the floor reflection, the other hand to her head above the right eye.

FOON SING is still. The others are still. They are looking at JANET.

What're you looking at?
Stop looking.
Stop looking!

FOON SING
(*goes to her to comfort, help her up*) <u>Things will get better.</u>

JANET
(*scuttles away from him, still on the floor*) Get away!

FOON SING
First come I work in laundry. Things hard for me also.

JANET
Don't talk to me!

FOON SING
Small shop. Wash, press, iron, laundry hard work. Not here. In Moose Jaw where uncle work on railway.

JANET
Moose Jaw?

FOON SING
Not a lie. Name of place, Moose Jaw. This is better.

JANET
(getting up) Eavesdropping is not better! Eavesdropping is bad! Do you know what eavesdropping is?

FOON SING
You talk out loud, how someone not hear?

JANET
I know all about you!

FOON SING
You know me?

JANET
You. Burn babies, white babies,

FOON SING
Oh. You see that?

JANET
What do you mean?

FOON SING
I ask if you see me burn babies.

JANET
I read it! In books!

FOON SING
But who burn babies?

JANET
Chinamen! And in newspapers too!

FOON SING
Oh. Always true, eh? What you read. You read bout Moose Jaw?

JANET
No!

FOON SING
No. Nowhere to read Moose Jaw. No need to read. First I go to Moose Jaw, fourteen years old, work hard in laundry, leg and this arm broken when men attack Chinese in Moose Jaw.

JANET
Why?

FOON SING
Why?

JANET
Why? What did you do?

FOON SING
Many are beaten, almost die. What we do is dig, hide, burrow in, in earth, under earth, beneath buildings. Save ourselves.

JANET
Why did they do that, what did you do? *(A pause. FOON SING says nothing.)* Well you must have done something. *(pause)* I don't believe there is a place called Moose Jaw.

FOON SING
We burn babies. I, myself, I burn, oh eight or nine babies, I lose count after five. *(pause)* Miss Doris is not always right, but sometimes. You are pretty. But maybe not very bright. Maybe stupid. Maybe I burn you, eh?

JANET
Don't speak to me like that! In this household you are here *(illustrating his lower status, one hand over other hand)* and I am here. Understand? And you treat me with respect!

FOON SING
(illustrates one hand on top of other hand) Willie here, Nursie here? – and Mr. Clarke-Evans bossman – here? *(a hand on top of "Nursie" hand)*

JANET
I know what you're saying!

FOON SING
What?… Tell me, I say what?

> *The sound of a small hand bell ringing; FOON SING takes off his jacket and his vest.*

I say, we are not so different… Willie… Nursie… our place. *(The bell is rung again.)* Not so different… no…. Sorry.

> *FOON SING passes JANET his coat and vest. She refuses to take them. He drapes them over a wingback.*

> *The sound of the hand bell again and with it whispering voices permeate the space. The words tumble over each other. Light is diminishing as FOON SING*

joins WONG SIEN and ROBERT on the periphery. DORIS watches JANET as JANET moves closer to observe the three men. FOON SING removes the sheet from the crate and folds it. ROBERT places JANET's suitcase on the crate and opens it. It's empty. The men tilt up and reach under several of the bound chairs removing packages which they give to FOON SING to place in JANET's suitcase. They work quickly and efficiently, sometimes seen in silhouette as they move behind and between the translucent "walls." The voices are on tape and they repeat, resonate, and overlap during the action)

WONG SIEN
Things have been arranged

ROBERT
Have they

WONG SIEN
You don't have to worry

FOON SING
Where do you want it

ROBERT
Leave it here

WONG SIEN
Pack it up until it's ready to go.

ROBERT
When will that be

WONG SIEN
Soon. We hear you have a new one in your house.

ROBERT
That's right.

FOON SING
Should I start now

ROBERT
Why not

WONG SIEN
A nursemaid

ROBERT
Not to worry.

WONG SIEN
The wife is a concern.

ROBERT
Not to worry

WONG SIEN
You are responsible

ROBERT
I know that, I said don't worry, I understand.

> *The continually repeated and overlapped words constitute a murmur under the following DORIS/JANET dialogue which occurs as FOON SING completes filling the suitcase and gives the suitcase to ROBERT who gives it to WONG SIEN. WONG SIEN hands ROBERT an envelope. ROBERT opens it and thumbs through its contents.*

> *JANET's responses to DORIS are robot-like. JANET's attention is on the men, particularly FOON SING. DORIS is in one dimension; JANET in another. The murmur of voices gradually grows a bit in volume, as does DORIS's voice as she speaks over it until the "moment of silence" indicated in script. Light is changing.*

DORIS
Nettie! Nettie!

JANET
Yes ma'am

DORIS
A drink, Nettie!

JANET
Yes ma'am

DORIS
Are you happier now?

JANET
Now

DORIS
But you weren't when you first came here now were you, tell the truth!

JANET
Truth

DORIS
Don't call me ma'am!

JANET
Ma'am.

DORIS
You know I hate it. Ma'am ma'am ma'am ma'am that's what you call the Queen… or some old lady or… some – so call me… Miss Doris – and I'll call you… Nettie. There. We're friends.

> *The low murmur of voices stops. A moment of silence as ROBERT and WONG SIEN become aware of JANET observing them. FOON SING notices their awareness.*

I like you Nettie.

> *ROBERT smiles at JANET.*

JANET
Nettie

> *WONG SIEN moves away with the suitcase. FOON SING goes to his jacket and vest to put them back on. DORIS's attention shifts to FOON SING.*

ROBERT
Rosemary

JANET
for remembrance

ROBERT
Is sleeping.

JANET
Is crying, I hear her now.

DORIS
(to FOON SING) And you say I like you too, Miss Doris.

> *FOON SING finishes his meticulous buttoning of vest, his donning of jacket. He takes an empty glass from DORIS.*

> *ROBERT puts his arm around JANET. DORIS's focus is on FOON SING as he mixes her a drink.*

Where's my drink Nettie?

> *ROBERT smiles at JANET.*

ROBERT

She isn't here Doris.

DORIS

What?

ROBERT

She's out.

DORIS

No.

ROBERT

She's out with Rosie.

DORIS

Rosemary!

ROBERT

That's right. She's with Rosie and the league of Scottish nannies in the park.

DORIS

(looking at ROBERT and JANET) Not Rosie! Rosemary!

ROBERT

They're pushing prams and telling tales on mistresses and masters. *(drops his arm from JANET)* And what do you suppose they say about you, Doris?

DORIS

Don't call her that!

ROBERT

(taking the drink from FOON SING as FOON SING offers it to DORIS) Thank you Willie.

DORIS

Her name is Rosemary! It's a beautiful name! You call her that! Why can't you call her that you – don't call her Rosie it's ugly and common and I don't care what they say about me! I could tell them lots of things about you and if they talk about me what do you suppose they'd say about you! Why – why do you call her Rosie?

ROBERT

It's your mother's name isn't it? Not Rosemary, "Rosie." *(quotes in a Yorkshire accent)* "Down to the pub for a quick one?" So you come by it honestly, Doris. And after our wedding reception, and a few in the Yorkshire local, your uncle gave me a nudge and a wink, and told me ever since your da's death, and maybe before, *(grabs DORIS from behind, pressing her close, and giving several pelvic thrusts)* "a couple of fellas was pokin' your mum, and she encouraged them like, and he hoped it didn't run in the family, but he felt I surely ought to be warned." *(He releases her.)*

DORIS
But you married me didn't you? Oh and wasn't I lucky, made a real catch I did. Lowered yourself, did you, marrying me? Well surprise surprise! Least all I've got to hide is a poor boozy mum!

ROBERT
And that's exactly the kind of thing that worries me, Doris. Not your predisposition for drink or any adulterous schemes you might harbour. However you open your mouth and out slips the inference that I have something to hide. And that's slipping out more and more often. And to inappropriate people.

DORIS
I don't do anything I don't say anything I don't – why do you do this to me?

ROBERT
I suppose I lose patience.

DORIS
Why do you do it!

ROBERT
To get your attention. Now listen.

DORIS
No not going to listen no!

> *She covers her ears with her hands, and staggers away from him. He attempts to grab her. In attempting to evade him she trips and lands hard on the floor. FOON SING and JANET touched by light are watching. After a moment ROBERT takes a sip of his drink and kneels on one knee beside her.*

ROBERT
Are you listening, Doris?

DORIS
Yes.

ROBERT
Listen carefully.... This has to stop. It can't go on. You put all of us, Rosemary, me, and you, in a very awkward position. Your behaviour draws attention to things. People outside our circle of friends begin to ask questions.

DORIS
What people?

ROBERT

I'm talking Doris. You're listening. Even our friends, good friends with whom we often do business, worry about your behaviour. And our business doings and dealings cannot withstand close scrutiny. Our friends protect us, but that protection is not infinite. We had to leave England because our partners there were careless. People started to talk. Moderation in all things was forgotten. People got Hurt. And now – we can't go back to England without my talking to people I don't want to talk to. Do you want us to have to leave here? Pick up and start all over again. Where would you like to live then? Vladivostok?

DORIS

It's not a nice business we're in.

ROBERT

You seem happy enough with the profits and product.

DORIS

You've got to help me.

ROBERT

You've got to help yourself. (*He lifts her face up, palm under her chin, forefinger and thumb on each side of her face, squeezing a little too hard so she must meet his eyes.*) No more. Of anything. Mmmn? Is that clear? Not any more. Or else something very bad will happen. And we don't want that do we? We don't want that.

> *He stands up, goes to the drinks table as lighting expands, drinks the last of the drink, sets the glass down, smiles at JANET.*

Hello Nettie. We've people coming. Get her up will you? (*watching as JANET helps DORIS up and off with her dressing gown, lays it on a chair*) That's a good girl... Nettie. You didn't like Nursie? Not too original was it. Sounds like a... matronly sort. (*speaking to FOON SING*) Not at all like her. First time I saw her—in London—when she answered the ad, I thought... where's her dress, Willie?

> *FOON SING gets a dress for DORIS and assists JANET in dressing DORIS.*

(*to JANET*) You've heard the naming of Willie story no doubt. Doris trots it out on a regular basis. I don't think Nursie's so bad. Maybe it's me. Wanting my way in everything. Always had it that way. Pity to change. Don't you think?... Eh?

JANET

I wouldn't know, Mr. Clarke-Evans.

ROBERT

Too formal, Nettie, much too formal.

Sound of 20s Charleston music, clink of glasses, murmur of party voices creeps in; the music will gradually increase in volume.

Willie calls me bossman, eh Willie? Mr. Clarke-Evans bossman. My friends call me C.E.... my mother calls me Robert... my business... associates... call me a number of names... what would you like to call me Nettie?... Choose. It's up to you.... Choose.... Something less formal?

A moment between JANET and ROBERT which he breaks off.

Feeling better, Doris?

DORIS
Much.

ROBERT
Let's have a look.

She smiles and steps forward for inspection. JANET and FOON SING await approval of their work. ROBERT adjusts a strand of her hair, looks again, minor adjustment to the dress.

Beautiful darling. Absolutely lovely.

DORIS
Just for you. And all your important people.

ROBERT
Yes indeed, we've got quite the crowd tonight.

They move arm in arm to the upstage periphery area. Their backs are to us as they meet and greet the unseen people. JANET and FOON SING are downstage looking out, viewing the scene that's taking place behind them. Lights are changing; shadows and light whirl and dip with a mirror-ball effect. JANET and FOON SING enjoy this glimpse of the elite.

FOON SING
Big party. You like it? *(JANET nods.)* Important people here. Governor's son.

JANET
Where?

FOON SING
There.... Almost fall down.... There. Big newspaper man... his wife there... much money, power, all here, Mr. Bossman's friends. Many of them here. You can read names in newspaper tomorrow.

JANET
I... I looked it up. On a map. Moose Jaw.

Pause.

So. I suppose, it does exist, Moose Jaw.

Pause.

So maybe – oh look – oh oops! Who's that, is that the

FOON SING
Governor's son. Lieutenant Governor. Tomorrow we find him. Still here. On bathroom floor or under bed.

JANET
No.

FOON SING
Yes.

JANET
Whose bed?

FOON SING
Shhh. He will be very pale. Not look good. Yes, there's money here… there's politics… big lawyer there…. Mr. Clarke-Evans is a man with many friends.

ROBERT and DORIS start to Charleston.

JANET
What's he do?

FOON SING
Do? Mmmmn – called Charleston.

JANET
I know that, I mean he goes to work doesn't he, what's he do?

FOON SING
He… he is moving things, you like the party?

JANET
It's wonderful.

FOON SING begins to Charleston. Lights begin to dim.

FOON SING
Like picture in book. Eh?

JANET joins FOON SING in the Charleston. They're facing front down stage while ROBERT and DORIS are upstage, facing upstage, doing the Charleston.

The dance is fun. The music begins to grow in volume; it speeds up, as does the dance. The dance and music move to a frantic pace. JANET and FOON SING whirl round and round faster and faster. Everything stops with a flash of blinding light. Snap to black.

A match is struck and a stick of incense is lit by WONG SIEN who is standing by the crate and chair. He sticks the incense in a rice bowl on the crate.

FOON SING is sitting in the chair behind the crate.

WONG SIEN
They have appointed me, Wong Sien, court interpreter. Wong Sien has good references from important people. I speak the court's words to defendant Foon Sing, and Foon Sing listens. When Foon Sing speaks, I speak his words in answer to the court. Court says Chinese are heathen. No Christian oath for heathens. For you, Foon Sing, the Fire Oath. These *(holding up several sheets of parchment)* are words I tell them you have told me. *(He lights the paper on fire.)* As they burn you swear to tell the truth or disgrace fall on ancestors. And then—just to be sure—court will give you chopping knife. And chicken. You will take knife in right hand *(he holds up knife in right hand)* chicken in left *(he holds up empty left hand)* Again Foon Sing, you swear to tell the truth… Remember who speaks for you Foon Sing. Who saves you in Moose Jaw. Who knows every thing.

He swiftly drops left hand to top of crate and brings the knife down on the crate, a resounding and loud thud and blackout.

A match flares as DORIS lights a cigarette. The suitcase is now sitting on the crate. The men are on the periphery. JANET is watching as DORIS scans the room but doesn't take in JANET's presence. A brush of the wind chimes. DORIS hearing the wind chimes quickly butts out the cigarette. She listens but hearing no further sound, she bends down near a wingback chair, runs her hand under it, gets up, goes to a side table, opens a drawer, feels inside, nothing. She turns on a table lamp. She looks round at the furniture as if gauging where to look next. She moves to the second wingback chair, she feels under it, up in the springs. She sees JANET and in a rush to stand she tips the chair over.

DORIS
Shhhh, shush, shosh, it's alright, a chair, it's just a chair Nettie. It just… it just… went over. But it's alright. We'll make it right. We will yes we will…

DORIS leaves the wingback and continues her search of the furniture (not the mirror wingbacks) eventually moving to the bound chairs on the periphery. JANET moves to the fallen wingback but doesn't right it as she gets caught up in watching DORIS.

You help me and… everything… will be… alright. There. There's an awful lot of it, isn't there. Chairs you know, just chairs. Don't you wonder? I know I would. I'd wonder… I need, no…. But I'd wonder and I and I wouldn't blame you if you did. Wonder. No I wouldn't. Don't ask! Shhhhhhh. And don't tell. It's…. Robert you see. It's his business. Import. And export. Furniture. Import and export of – Furniture! To all sorts of places. From Switzerland. And and France. From France and then it goes to oh, lots of places…. Oh!

She sees the suitcase on top of the crate. She stretches her hand towards it but doesn't touch it, wants to move towards it but doesn't.

This!… This is!… this is just for here! For sale! Here! It will be – Leaving…. Soon. Yes. Because.

Pause.

Oh Nettie. Don't ask. Don't tell.

She starts to cry.

Do you think you could help me Nettie?

JANET
With what?

DORIS
Don't tell. I was – I was looking for something but – not with that no. No help with that, no no no.

JANET
It's alright. *(making a move to comfort her)*

DORIS
No it isn't.

JANET
It's alright. *(helping her into the upright wingback)*

DORIS
I'm not a bad person. Robert thinks that I'm bad but I'm not. He is, it's him! No not really but sometimes–

She draws back from JANET'S embrace so she can look JANET in the face.

I'm not myself Nettie. Could you…

She stares into JANET's face. DORIS tilts her head slightly as if in an effort to see JANET clearly. She takes JANET's face in both hands, draws it close.

Could you…. You're a very pretty girl. Has anyone told you that?

> DORIS kisses JANET on the forehead then suddenly, impulsively, pushes JANET violently to the floor.

Has He told you that?

> Her hands are twisting her dress, she looks down at the fabric and is disturbed by it.

What's this, what is it, get it off me, get it off me get it off off!

> She pulls off her dress throwing it on the floor.

There. I want my robe Have you seen my robe? Get my Robe! I want—

> She finds her robe on the upset wingback, picks it up and puts it on.

Yes. Yes. My, my robe. My – yes, I want—

> She puts her hand in the pocket of her robe and stops talking. After a moment she withdraws her hand, looks at something in her hand.

It's… all right then. (She puts her hand back in her pocket.) There. I… I feel better now. It's alright…. Do you know what I'm going to do?

I'm going to go to bed now.
Thank you Nettie.
Good night.

> DORIS moves away to curl up on one of the bound chairs.

Good night Nettie.

> FOON SING, ROBERT and WONG SIEN are watching JANET, each from a different position. The wind chime is stirred by a light wind as JANET's gaze turns to a wingback chair. JANET feels under it to see what DORIS was looking for. Nothing there. She feels beside the cushion of the chair, nothing there. She looks towards her suitcase on the crate. She is drawn to the suitcase, gets it, and brings it downstage to open it. The interior of the suitcase is a white, luxurious material. There's no sign of the packages. The suitcase is empty except for a handgun. JANET takes the gun out. The wind will gradually die away with the random residual sound of the wind chimes.

ROBERT
Willie!

> JANET quickly closes the suitcase and hides the gun behind her back as she turns to watch ROBERT approach.

See to that!

FOON SING
(*going to the suitcase*) This... this – Willie leave out. Not thinking. Nursie... not looking... just... find. This is fault of Willie.

ROBERT
Thank you Willie. (*He rights the upturned wingback.*)

FOON SING
All Willie. His fault. Not Nursie!

ROBERT
You can go now.

> *After a momentary hesitation FOON SING leaves to place the suitcase on the periphery. He picks up the sheet that had covered the chair by the crate and folds it as he watches.*

(*turns on a table lamp and gazes at JANET for a moment before speaking*) How... is... Rosemary, Nettie?...

JANET
She's alright.

ROBERT
Sleeping I hope. Because it's very very late. You're up very late, Nettie. Is Rosemary sleeping?

JANET
Yes sir.

ROBERT
And Doris?

JANET
Sleeping.

ROBERT
Perhaps. How about you, are you having problems with sleeping?

JANET
Me? No sir.

ROBERT
Yet here you are. Looking for something, were you?

JANET
No sir. (*She casually reveals the gun.*)

ROBERT
Which leaves us with what?

JANET
I thought I heard someone, voices, moving – I thought I'd come down and...

ROBERT
You thought you'd come down and... and what?

JANET
And... there was... nobody, here sir. Must have been dreaming.

ROBERT
And the gun, where did you find it?

JANET
There were a few things left in my suitcase sir and–

ROBERT
There's no need for the sir.

JANET
It looked like my suitcase and since I was up–

ROBERT
With a few things on your mind you searched out a suitcase and, voila!

JANET
Just as you say.

ROBERT
May I? (*He holds out his hand for the gun. She suddenly points the gun at him.*)
Other way round please!

JANET
Is it loaded?

> ROBERT *makes a grab for it, she lifts it out of his reach, then slowly brings it*
> *back down, the barrel pointing at his head, his chest, his groin, till she turns it,*
> *grip towards his hand, and offers it to him. He takes it from her. She laughs*
> *and starts to leave. He moves around in front of her blocking her exit and*
> *draws her back into the room. She is aware now of the gun in his hand*
> *although he makes no overt threat with it.*

ROBERT
You could have harmed yourself Nettie!... You must be careful when you're
looking for things. There're a lot of things in this house. From the war you
know. Potentially dangerous things. Souvenirs. Like the gun and. Other
things.... Would you care for a drink Nettie?

JANET
I don't think so.

ROBERT
A nightcap with me. As a favour?…

JANET
Well

ROBERT
It's been a long time…

JANET
Well

ROBERT
I insist.

JANET
Alright then.

ROBERT
(He pours her a drink, but not one for himself. He gives her the drink, indicates she should sit, and toys with the gun as he speaks.) Yes. Did you know I flew planes? The Great War. I flew a plane called the Spad. You know who you're looking at Nettie? At a man who's killed men. And who himself was The Red Baron's fortieth kill. Drink up…. And after the war, married my beautiful Doris, and set up in business. I suppose… I have the Red Baron to thank for it all, my encounter with him led me to Doris, and… indirectly I'd say… into business.

JANET
What – sort of business?

ROBERT
What sort of business? Why the pharmaceutical business, Nettie, I – thought you knew.

JANET
Import and export?

ROBERT
Oh you are a clever girl.

JANET
I thought it was furniture.

ROBERT
Import and export… of furniture too. *(noticing DORIS' dress on the floor)* You've been talking to Doris?

JANET
Every day sir.

ROBERT
There's that sir again. We'll have to do something about it. When I met you, in London, the hotel room in London, and after, I thought…

JANET
What?

ROBERT
What did you think?… Come on, you can tell me.

A slow light change, which when complete gives an impression of caged or entrapment.

JANET
I thought… you were a very nice man.

ROBERT
But did you like me?

JANET
Or I'd not've taken the job.

ROBERT
The job… I liked you. Or I'd not have offered the job. I acted on impulse you see. Passion, yes, saw that in your eyes.

JANET
I wouldn't think you'd want much of that in a nursemaid.

ROBERT
Some say it's essential. Now with you, it flares up every once in a while. The question is, should you suppress it? It can take you places…

JANET
I don't think so.

ROBERT
Another drink?

JANET
I don't really drink sir. *(starts to leave)*

ROBERT
Janet!

ROBERT points the gun directly at her for a brief moment and she stops her exit. He motions her back with the gun, but seems to use it as an extension of his hand seemingly unaware of it and the threat it poses. JANET is aware of the threat.

Did you think we were finished? I crave company, Janet. Oh look, there by your feet. My wife's dress…. Just look at that. Left where she dropped it. Expensive and new. Gorgeous too, don't you think?

JANET
It's very pretty.

ROBERT
Do you like it?

JANET
It's very nice.

ROBERT
Go on, pick it up, try it on.

JANET
I don't really want to.

ROBERT
And you don't really drink. Go on… I'm giving it to you.

JANET
I couldn't take Miss Doris' clothes.

ROBERT
Obviously Doris doesn't care for the dress. And it's mine to give. After all, I paid for it. Pick it up!

JANET picks it up, then makes a sudden run to exit. This time ROBERT gets in front of her, pointing the gun directly at her. He forces her back.

Try it on.

JANET
No.

Pause.

ROBERT
Willie! Come here Willie.

FOON SING approaches carrying the folded sheet.

ROBERT sits in a wingback at ease but the gun is directly threatening JANET now. An almost subliminal slow drum of a heartbeat accompanied by the sound of blood moving through chambers and channels sneaks in under dialogue. This sound continues under the dialogue. The sound grows slightly more present during the scene, but again is almost more felt than heard.

Nursie needs some help with her buttons. Do you think you could help her? *(Pause, as FOON SING hesitates.)* We've been talking. About war. About guns. How dangerous they are. About.... Business.... And Passion. In a roundabout way.

DORIS uncurls from the bound chair and observes the scene. WONG SIEN is a constant observer.

And about Curiosity in a roundabout way. And in a tiny way, about my wife. And I've given the lovely dress my wife's discarded, to Nursie. And she's accepted. I believe. And now I'd like to see it on her. *(gesturing with the gun)* If you lift your arms Nursie I think Willie can...

FOON SING makes no move to assist.

Go on Willie. What do I pay you for?

The gun shifts momentarily to FOON SING and he puts the sheet on a mirror wingback.

Up with the arms!

JANET lifts her arms. FOON SING moves to JANET and pulls the apron coverall off.

Does your dress do up the back?... Try to reach.... Go on. Try. You must when you're all alone. I've never known how women do it.... They need a man. Or someone like Willie.... Come on! It's late! Past my bedtime! Let's hurry shall we!

FOON SING undoes her dress. He stops. ROBERT gives a small jerk with the gun, and FOON SING pushes it off her shoulders so it falls to the floor around her feet.

And the slip...

FOON SING steps away from JANET.

The slip Willie!

FOON SING
A good servant speaks when it is necessary.

ROBERT aims the gun more directly at each of them in turn.

photo: Charles Hope Photography

l to r: Jarvis Hall, Jovanni Sy, Daniela Vlaskalic.

ROBERT
Eeany… meany… miney… moe

With "moe" the gun ends up pointing at FOON SING. Pause.

FOON SING
This is not necessary.

ROBERT cocks the gun. JANET removes her slip.

She is not a danger.

ROBERT
What would you bet on that, Willie?

FOON SING
My life.

ROBERT shifts the gun to point at JANET.

ROBERT
No Willie. Her life.

FOON SING passes JANET her apron coverall and stands so as to block ROBERT's view of her.

FOON SING
I will see to her.

ROBERT
Do that! *(pause)* Well… I'm sorry, Nettie.

He puts the gun down on the bar table. He smiles at JANET.

I misunderstood. If you didn't want the dress – you – had only to say so…. Good night.

He leaves, meeting DORIS on the upstage periphery. JANET throws down the apron. FOON SING and JANET watch as ROBERT kisses DORIS on the mouth. JANET walks to the bar table, picks up the gun.

JANET
Robert!!

He and DORIS turn to look at her. JANET aims the gun at them directly upstage.

FOON SING
Noooo!

As WONG SIEN is speaking and moving from the periphery, the following action occurs: JANET whirls round from facing upstage with the gun to face downstage. The gun is now pointing directly downstage into the audience as JANET faces them. FOON SING picks up the sheet from the mirror wingback chair, comes up behind JANET, enfolding her in the sheet. It covers her extended arm and hand holding the gun, completely envelopes her body as she resists.

WONG SIEN

If you fire gun three times eighteen inches from head of slaughtered pig! Powder burns on pig! Bullets shatter! Skull is intact!

If you fire gun three times ten inches from head severed for this purpose from unclaimed dead pauper! Powder burns on face of this poor person! Bullets shatter! Skull intact!

FOON SING overpowers JANET who ceases to resist collapsing on the floor. FOON SING kneels down beside her. Light is isolating the two and WONG SIEN.

But! Bullet found in basement laundry room of Mr. Clarke-Evans is pristine. Not Shattered. *(He looks down at JANET and FOON SING.)* No Powder Burns mark victim's face. Entry wound from gunshot is above victim's right eye. Width of wound is three eighths of inch. Skull Is Fractured, as if struck by heavy blow. Scalp is ripped from underlying bone. Almost detached.

Sound stops.

(addresses the audience) Testimony of Foon Sing, only other person in house at time of death is: this person kill them self. These are the words of Foon Sing. I speak them as Court Interpreter. Foon Sing says: This Person Kill Them Self!

Very loud resonant sound of blow from gavel. Blackout.

l to r: Anthony Chan, Laura Parken, Jarvis Hall, Daniela Vlaskalic, Jovanni Sy.

photo: Charles Hope Photography

Act Two

Charleston music playing. A light illuminates only FOON SING's face. He is looking directly out front. We stay with FOON SING's face established in the only source of light in the blackness as the music plays. FOON SING appears to be alone. The music is fading as he speaks.

FOON SING
Foon Sing find Missy on floor.... Foon Sing find Missy on floor.... She come down stairs in dark, it is late and dark. This is how it happens. She come downstairs in dark, she take bad step, and fall... I find her. This is true. I swear it.

JANET
No.

Light begins to grow on the rest of the room. DORIS, ROBERT, and WONG SIEN observe the scene in full or partial silhouette behind the translucent walls. JANET is sitting in a wingback chair, the sheet wrapped around her. FOON SING moves to her.

FOON SING
I find you–

JANET
Not like that.

FOON SING
Hit your head maybe. You have a bad fall. Many times Foon Sing do same thing but – catch myself.

JANET
Not true!

FOON SING
You must – catch yourself. When you come near that bad place catch yourself. Stop!

JANET
Where're my clothes?

FOON SING
You must stop!

JANET
Stop what?

FOON SING
I try to stop you, catch you falling, and two will fall!

JANET
(*stands up*) Where're my clothes?

> Pause. JANET opens the sheet draped around her and glances down. She is
> fully dressed. She looks at FOON SING who says nothing. She looks at her
> hand, flexing it slightly as if gripping a gun, finger on trigger. She points it at
> FOON SING.

Where is it?

FOON SING
Where is what?

> JANET drops the sheet and goes to the bar table where ROBERT had left the
> gun.

You must rest.

> FOON SING picks up the sheet and begins folding it. There is no gun on the
> bar table. JANET scans the room, and then fixes on a wingback chair DORIS
> had been sitting in. She moves towards it.

Why look, nothing there.

> She runs her hand round between the cushion and the arm of the chair. She
> comes up with DORIS' cigarette case. She holds it up.

JANET
Nothing?

> Abrupt light change. Long slow exhalation of a flute under the following:

FOON SING
(*plucking the case from JANET's hand*) Stop.

> The sound of a bang on a wooden door.

> FOON SING moves to the periphery, leaving the sheet on a mirror wingback.
> He takes off his jacket and vest. He opens the suitcase. He tilts several bound
> chairs over and removes packages from the frames of each chair placing
> the packages in the suitcase. JANET follows FOON SING to the periphery
> watching. As she is speaking DORIS moves out from behind the wall.

JANET
I see you. You think I don't? I do. I'm watching yes I am... I'm watching you!

> DORIS is wearing no shoes and the party dress from Act One. The light is
> changing. The flute is beginning to fade away. She puts her hands on JANET's
> shoulders, whispers in her ear.

DORIS
What're you looking at, Nettie? *(She starts to sway, swaying JANET with her.)*
Ooooh I see what you're looking at, Nettie,
I've looked at him too,
But he simply won't do,
Out of bounds Nettie,
Verboten!

> *She quickly turns JANET around, to face her, her hands grasping JANET's upper arms, and her face in JANET's face.*

What're you thinking 'bout Nettie?!
I've thought of it too.
That
Makes me
And makes you–

> *She suddenly throws her arms up in the air and shrieks.*

Ooohhh!!!

> *She grabs JANET's hand, places it on her shoulders, places her own hand around JANET's waist, grabs JANET's other hand, forcing JANET into a position as her dance partner. DORIS sings and dances, manipulating JANET's participation as she were a big doll or puppet.*

You beautiful doll, you great big beautiful doll!
Let me put my arms about you,
I could never live without you,
Oh! You beautiful doll, you great big beautiful doll!
If you ever leave me how my heart will ache,
I want to hug you but I fear you'd break.
Oh! Oh! Oh! Oh! Oh You–
Look.

> *She quickly turns JANET around to face FOON SING as we snap to black.*

> *Lights up on FOON SING in silhouette behind the translucent wall. The light shifts back and forth as if cast by a swinging light bulb. Two men in silhouette are beating FOON SING. We hear taped voices of several men permeating and filling the space, along with the sounds of their exertion and of FOON SING's reaction to the beating.*

VOICES
Hit him.... Hit him again!... Make him sign.... Kill him!... Who's got the paper?... Talk!... Come on talk!... Talk!... Don't be a fool.... Sign!... We know who did it.... Talk!... Get the rope... You're gonna die Willie

The dialogue doesn't stop for the following action: One of the men slips a noose round FOON SING's neck. The other man shoves FOON SING onto his knees. The man yanks the rope up; FOON SING's neck is extended.

VOICES

We know it's not you.... Give us the bossman, Willie.... It's not worth it Willie

The second man holds a gun to FOON SING's head.

VOICES

Who did it.... Talk Willie.... Talk!... Talk!... Do it!

A loud resonant sound with blackout. The start of FOON SING slumping is caught in the mini-second before black.

Light up on DORIS and JANET as DORIS flips JANET back around to face her, grabbing JANET's hands, leaning out at something like a 45 degree angle and whirling herself and JANET around.

DORIS

And around and around and around and around and around

JANET

Let me go! Let me go! Stop!

DORIS stops. DORIS is out of breath and dishevelled. DORIS gives JANET a vigorous push. From the floor JANET looks up to see FOON SING who, in a brush of light upstage, is righting the bound chairs. ROBERT is beside him, overseeing, and smoking a cigarette. WONG SIEN is checking the suitcase. During the following scene ROBERT and WONG SIEN are at ease on the periphery. FOON SING will step behind a wall where he is unseen. He will put on his vest and jacket.

DORIS

What are you doing!... I said, what're you doing!

JANET

Nothing

DORIS

Nothing ma'am.

JANET

I'm not doing anything ma'am.

DORIS

Well hadn't you ought to be doing something? Isn't that what we hired you for? To do things? Rosemary things, those things, and things for me, yes, things for me and for Robert too. This is a busy household Nettie and you can't expect

l to r: Anthony Chan, Jovanni Sy, Jarvis Hall.   *photo: Charles Hope Photography*

Willie to do it all! I'd hate to dismiss you Nettie. I don't have to tell you, without a good reference from me, or from Robert, I don't know where you'd find work in the city. And with the money you owe for your passage

JANET
I'm paying it back, ma'am, most of it's paid.

DORIS
We've incurred other expenses.

JANET
What expenses?

DORIS
I can't go into it now.

JANET
(getting up) But I need to know!

DORIS
Room and board for one.

JANET
Room and board?

DORIS
It all adds up. I can't talk now, you've upset me Nettie! I'm all upset. And... and where are my shoes? You've lost my shoes.... You've stolen my shoes!

JANET
I haven't.

DORIS
Yes you have.

JANET
No.

DORIS
You find them. Find them!

> *JANET looks for the shoes.*

They were my favourite pair.

JANET
They haven't been lost.

DORIS
  I know!

JANET
  They're here somewhere.

DORIS
  I know!

JANET
  I didn't steal them, you just–!

DORIS
  Just what? I said what!

JANET
  Nothing

DORIS
  What!

JANET
  Nothing!

DORIS
  Thief! Liar!

JANET
  Here, here, I found them they're here. *(finding a pair of red shoes, goes to pass them to DORIS and stops)* But – these aren't her favourite pair–

> *DORIS slaps JANET's face. DORIS sits in a wingback chair. Lights slowly begin to change.*

DORIS
  Put them on!

> *She thrusts out her hands and JANET puts a shoe on each hand.*

Like a glass slipper Nettie…. Two glass slippers…. Was it one or two slippers she lost at the Ball?… Which was it Nettie?

JANET
  (sitting in the second wingback) I don't know.

DORIS
  Well you should. You're a nursemaid aren't you? When Rosemary asks what will you say?

JANET
I don't know

DORIS
That'll be very distressing for her. It's very distressing for me. (*looking at her shoes on her hands*) Are these red?
No they aren't red.
Ma'am, always say ma'am.
Tell me the story of the red shoes, Nettie, I hope you know that one.

JANET
Which one

DORIS
My favourite, the story of the – what? The what?

JANET
Red shoes.

A dry rattling sound is heard faintly at random intervals.

DORIS
That's right. And how does it begin?

JANET
Once... upon a time?

DORIS
Yes, that's right, go on.

JANET
a little girl

DORIS
a poor little girl who had nothing, not even a mother

JANET
had a... pair of red shoes

DORIS
Red ragged shoes – and?

JANET
and she...

DORIS
was walking

DORIS begins to slowly move the shoes to illustrate the story. The light will get fainter isolating DORIS and JANET. They are close together in the two wingback chairs. The dry rattle sounds at intervals.

JANET
was walking

DORIS
in the woods one day when a very rich lady came by, swept the little girl up, dressed her in the best of clothes, and burnt the red ragged shoes. What happened then?

JANET
She bought her new shoes

DORIS
Yes. Black shoes. *(or whatever the colour of JANET's shoes)* But that little girl by conniving and cunning got herself a pair of...

JANET
Red shoes

DORIS
Yes, beautiful red shoes, shoes made for dancing, red dancing shoes, and the little girl started to dance in those shoes and she danced and she danced but when she wanted to stop, she found that she couldn't. The right shoe kept dancing while she pulled at the left and the left shoe kept dancing while she pulled at the right. Next thing you know those red shoes danced her out of the light and into the dark and out of the house and into the woods and out of the woods and over the hills and down the hills and into the alleys and she begged them to stop but they wouldn't. The red shoes kept dancing through forests and streams in the wind and the rain and the snow. She got ever so tired and filled with fear when one day who should come upon her dancing but a man with his axe in the woods. A man with his axe in the woods. She said please please cut off the straps of my shoes! So he tried, but he couldn't. Then she said please please cut off my feet. So he did. And those feet in the red shoes went dancing dancing dancing. Dancing on out of sight.

And the girl. Became a servant. And lived. At the beck and call of others. A poor crippled girl. Till the day that she died.

Dry rattle sound stops. Silence.

DORIS holds her hands out to JANET offering the shoes. JANET takes each shoe carefully off DORIS' hands, and holds the shoes in her lap.

(She gets up to leave.) Where's Willie?

JANET
> (*whispers*) I don't know

DORIS
> Where is Willie?

JANET
> (*whispers*) I'm not sure.

DORIS
> Other things are missing, Nettie. Have you seen my silver case? (*She moves to a chair on the periphery and stops.*) I'd like it back Nettie! (*She sits on one of the bound chairs and watches JANET.*)

> *Oriental music, a minimalist sound, is heard faintly. JANET considers the shoes. After a moment she puts them on her feet. She tries them out, slowly standing up in them, taking a few steps.*

JANET
> Here. Anywhere here. (*whirling around*) Anywhere I want to go.

> *She begins to dance, a simple flowing movement. She is caught in the act by WONG SIEN's voice. He moves from the periphery and during his speech tracks her as she attempts to continue her dance. The dance soon fragments, disintegrates as he more aggressively stalks, and then blocks her movement confining her to a small circle and stillness by the end of his speech.*

WONG SIEN
> (*to JANET*) Seven days after inquest men with hoods seize Foon Sing at night, take him to abandoned house. Shackle his feet to bolt in floor, hold him in darkened room. Six weeks of this captivity. He is beaten with clubs. His scalp is split. His eyes are blackened. He loses hearing permanently in one ear. They choke him with rope. They threaten him with gun. They ask who fired gun!
>
> Foon Sing says person kill them self.
> They say Foon Sing must sign paper with the name of killer.
> Foon Sing say person kill them self.
> They say we know business in that house, give us the bossman! You go free!
> Foon Sing say person kill them self!
> Hooded men say finish it! They take Foon Sing to field, they say we execute you here!
> Foon Sing say nothing.
> Hooded men leave Foon Sing. Throw him away in ditch. He find his way back to road. Police find Foon Sing. Take him to jail! Charge Him with murder!
>
> This is Foon Sing's story!

WONG SIEN looks towards the periphery. FOON SING enters from between the walls. He's wearing his jacket and vest. A more crystalline variation of the music plays faintly as FOON SING approaches JANET. He is concealing something behind his back. JANET watches him. Somewhat formally he presents her with a cube-shaped red gift box. She takes it, and holds it. FOON SING opens it and gives it back to her. She looks in the box and smiles, takes the top from FOON SING and replaces it on the box. She gives him back the box, a hand on the top and on the bottom of the box. He takes it from her placing his hand over hers on the top and bottom of the box. He exits with the box between the walls. The music stops.

(to audience) Thirteen are charged with being, and helping, men in hoods. Include important lawyer appointed by Attorney General as Special Counsel in murder case, two police commissioners, one chief constable, one detective sergeant, one chairman of Police Commission. All charged with kidnapping miserable Chinese man?…

All go to trial!
Kidnapping case – Dismissed!
All go free.

Approaching ROBERT and speaking to him.

But how do hooded men talk to Foon Sing during kidnap? Make sure he understand their threats. They need interpreter. Where to find good interpreter? Wong Sien! Me! Myself! I am Good Interpreter. Recommended by important men. Sooo… I am there as Good Interpreter in Court although I was also there with hooded men who kidnap.

JANET watches as ROBERT counts money into WONG SIEN's hand.

Never charged though.

WONG SIEN picks up the suitcase, which FOON SING has packed.

Funny world, heh? Good joke.

He puts the suitcase on the crate, opens it, and counts the packets.

<u>One two three four five six seven eight nine… nine?… Nine!…</u> One is missing!

ROBERT
Willie!

A loud ka-thud and a wave of low muttering voices fills the space with dim and shadowy light. FOON SING joins ROBERT as WONG SIEN slams the suitcase shut.

In the darkness JANET crouches down to avoid being seen as the beam of a flashlight dips and dives behind the walls. It's carried by ROBERT and his voice is heard calling out over the muttering voices.

Who's there!… Come on! Come out. Who's there!… Willie, the gun, get the gun…. Careful…. Who's there!

The flickering light reveals FOON SING and ROBERT moving cautiously behind the walls searching for an intruder.

JANET slips her shoes off and as she makes a move to the left, ROBERT enters with the flashlight. She dodges to the right and sees the shadowy figure of FOON SING carrying a gun. JANET moves to a wingback chair and quickly hides the shoes thrusting them down between the cushion and the side of the chair. The beam of the flashlight catches JANET on the floor by the chair. ROBERT approaches, focusing the light on JANET.

Nettie?… What're you doing?…

The beam from the flashlight picks out FOON SING with the gun, without jacket or vest and in his sock feet.

It's only Nursie, Willie. You can put that away. (*The flashlight returns to JANET.*) We thought you were an intruder, Nettie. You know you can't go wandering about the house at night. Anything could happen.

* *REPEAT 1 refers to following scene.*

There is a heavy loud ker-chunk sound as ROBERT turns on the side table lamp. Light pops up in the room accompanied by a low dull drone, almost subliminal, which continues under dialogue.

Light reveals JANET on the floor by the wingback chair; FOON SING putting the gun down on the side table by that wingback chair; ROBERT putting the flashlight down on the side table by the second wingback chair. On that side table sits the lamp he has just turned on. DORIS and WONG SIEN are watching from the periphery.

JANET
I could trip and fall?

ROBERT
Perhaps, yes.

JANET starts to get up to leave.

Nettie. (*She stops.*) We need to talk.

JANET
Now?

ROBERT
As good a time as any. Sit Nettie, pick a chair.

JANET looks at the chair in which she's hidden the shoes and sits.

How're you feeling?

JANET
Fine.

ROBERT
Not having problems sleeping?

JANET
Why do you keep asking me that?

ROBERT
It's just that… on a number of occasions late at night, we find you up and about, and I suppose we wonder why. We're worried about you, Nettie.

JANET
I can take care of myself.

ROBERT
Now that's the thing we're beginning to wonder about… and if you can't take care of yourself—don't speak, hear me out—if you can't take care of yourself… is it reasonable—or rational—to expect you to care for Rosemary?

JANET
(gets up) So I'll give my notice. I'll go right now, I don't care how much I owe you.

ROBERT
What do you owe?

JANET
Nothing – so there's nothing keeping me. So.

ROBERT
It's the middle of the night Nettie.

JANET
I'm going.

The low almost subliminal drone swells.

She starts off. As she passes ROBERT, he reaches out gently catching her arm with one hand. She stops and looks at him. He draws her to him. He kisses her neck. She begins undoing the buttons of her blouse. During this her gaze is fixed on FOON SING. She's smiling.

Blackout, then immediately:

* REPEAT 2 refers to following scene.

There is a heavy loud ker-chunk sound as ROBERT turns on the side table lamp.

Light pops up in the room accompanied by a low dull drone, almost subliminal, which continues under dialogue. The drone is more present than in REPEAT 1.

Light reveals JANET on the floor by the wingback chair; FOON SING putting the gun down on the side table by that wingback chair; ROBERT putting the flashlight down on the side table by the second wingback chair. On that side table sits the lamp he has just turned on. DORIS and WONG SIEN are watching from the periphery.

Everyone is in the identical positions as in REPEAT 1 but JANET's blouse is undone. The dialogue and action are more adversarial and quicker.

JANET
I could trip and fall?

ROBERT
Possibly yes.

JANET starts to get up to leave.

Nettie. (*She stops.*) We need to talk.

JANET
Now?

ROBERT
Sit Nettie,

JANET looks at the chair in which she's hidden the shoes and sits.

How're you feeling?

JANET
Fine.

ROBERT
>Having problems sleeping?

JANET
>Why do you keep asking me that!

ROBERT
>On occasion late at night, we find you up and about. We're worried about you, Nettie.

JANET
>I can take care of myself.

ROBERT
>Now that's the thing we're beginning to wonder about, and if you can't take care of yourself–

JANET
>(*getting up*) So I'll give my notice! I don't care how much I owe you!

ROBERT
>What do you owe?

JANET
>Nothing – I'm going!

>>*She starts off, ROBERT reaches out catching her arm with one hand, stopping her exit.*

ROBERT
>Doris tells me things have gone missing.

JANET
>If things are missing I'd look no further than her!

ROBERT
>Why's that Nettie?

JANET
>Because she takes it and hides it!

DORIS
>(*up from her chair on the periphery*) Who does?

JANET
>Who do you think?

DORIS
>Meaning me?

The drone swells.

JANET
Yes you! *(turning to ROBERT)* She's the one, her!

DORIS
(raising her arm and hand to deliver a blow to the back of JANET's head as she screams) Liar!

Blackout, then immediately:

* REPEAT 3 refers to following scene.

There is a heavy loud ker-chunk sound as ROBERT turns on the side table lamp. Light pops up in the room accompanied by a low dull drone, almost subliminal, which continues under dialogue. The drone is more present than in REPEAT 2.

Light reveals JANET on the floor by the wingback chair; FOON SING putting the gun down on the side table by that wingback chair; ROBERT putting the flashlight down on the side table by the second wingback chair. On that side table sits the lamp he has just turned on. DORIS and WONG SIEN are watching from the periphery.

Everyone is in the identical positions as in REPEAT 1 and 2. JANET's blouse is undone; her hair is in disarray. The dialogue and action are much more adversarial and quicker.

JANET
I could trip and fall.

ROBERT
Possibly. Sit!

JANET sits.

How're you feeling?

JANET
Fine!

ROBERT
No problems sleeping?

JANET
Don't keep asking me that!

ROBERT
We're worried about you!

JANET
I can take care of myself!

ROBERT
Can you?

JANET
(*getting up*) I don't care how much I owe!

ROBERT
Who do you owe?

JANET
I'm going

    She starts off, ROBERT grabs her arm, stopping her exit.

ROBERT
Things have gone missing.

JANET
She takes it and hides it!

DORIS
(*up from her chair*) Liar!

    FOON SING picks up the gun.

JANET
(*turning to ROBERT*) She's the one, her!

ROBERT
(*grabs JANET*) Hides what?

    The drone swells louder.

JANET
(*holds up her fingers and counts them off*) One two three four five six seven eight nine… nine?… nine?… one is missing. One is missing!

    WONG SIEN stands up as she's counting. He pushes up his sleeves.

ROBERT
(*still restraining JANET*) Willie!

    FOON SING puts the gun down on a side table, kneels by the chair where JANET had hidden the shoes. He puts his hand down the side of the chair, draws out a package. He holds up the package.

JANET breaks free of ROBERT and runs away only to be stopped by the sight of WONG SIEN who has a pair of stockings draped from his hands. The legs are splattered with blood; the feet are heavily bloodied.

WONG SIEN
These are bloody stockings worn by person who shoots himself. At time of death person is wearing shoes, and stockings. How does this blood come to be on feet of stockings, if shoes are on feet, at time of death?!

He holds up one hand. He opens his hand showing JANET the palm and blood runs from the upheld palm down his arm. He extends his hand outward towards JANET.

JANET
NOOOOO!

The drone increases in volume with JANET's scream and stops as her "No" stops. She stands alone, isolated, eyes shut, hands over ears.

There is an air of casual ease to DORIS, ROBERT and WONG SIEN as WONG SIEN wipes his arm and hand with the stockings and discards them, leaving them hanging over the side of the crate, and rolls down his sleeves

FOON SING goes to JANET and holds out his hand. She doesn't take it but he is able to draw her over to a wingback chair where she sits. Light increasingly isolates JANET and FOON SING. WONG SIEN, ROBERT and DORIS watch, brushed by light.

FOON SING
Shhhh. Shhhh. Now you must rest.

JANET takes FOON SING's hand and pulls him down to her. She whispers to him.

JANET
Get the gun Willie, we need the gun…. Do you want me to get it? I'll get it.

FOON SING
You're tired now.

JANET
We've got to help ourselves Willie because nobody else will help us. You were right, it is bad business and powerful friends and what can we do? I know what they're doing, and I know what they've done, everything that they've done, and it's not your fault Willie you're caught, and the two of us here, in this house, caught in this house.

FOON SING
Please… please it would be better if you'd sleep.

JANET

You heard what he said, obligated he said, yes, obligated to look after me, wouldn't dream of my leaving until they can see that I'm well. They think it's my head. It's not my head, Willie you know that. *(getting up)* It's what I know.

A low sound, drone-like, creeps it; it never gets very loud.

FOON SING

Rest now.

JANET

No rest Willie no. Tell me what I can do… tell me if we had the gun… what do you think I should do…. What do you think…

She is light-headed and almost faints. FOON SING catches her and lowers her to the floor.

My head… right here *(touches her head above her right eye)* right there… *(touches his head above his right eye)* does it hurt?

FOON SING

No.

JANET

(Her hand moves down to his cheek.) Doesn't hurt…. Colour of… honey… colour of… *(She takes his hand and presses it to her lips.)* sweet… like honey?

She opens his shirt and bends her head to kiss his chest. He holds her placing his hand on the back of her head.

WONG SIEN

Exit wound in back of the head measures one and one half inches in width. This should cause blow out. Much blood and tissue from the brain should blow out! Yet in basement laundry room, where body is found, there is no splattered blood, there is no brain tissue found. No blood! No tissue! No powder burn on face! Blood on stocking! Skull is shattered! Bullet is pristine! How could this happen?

FOON SING picks up JANET and places her in a wingback chair. He pushes her dress above her knees, kneels between her legs. She kisses him as they embrace. The low drone stops.

JANET

Get the gun.

He turns away from her but she traps him with her arms around his neck and he sits on the floor between her legs as she leans forward in the chair her arms around his neck.

JANET
> There, there… it will be alright, there there…

> *She hums the first two lines and then picks up the words on line three eventually fading out as her eyes close.*

Lullaby and good night
Those sweet eyes close tight
Bright angels are near
So sleep without fear
If God's will thou shalt wake
When the morning doth break
If God's will thou shalt…

> *When JANET stops singing we hear the lullaby being played very faintly and slowly with one finger on a tinkly piano the notes becoming more and more fragmented, further apart. The sound of the piano continues through the following:*

> *FOON SING gently lifts her arms from around his neck. JANET appears to be asleep. He takes the sheet he'd picked up at the beginning of the act and places it over her, like a blanket.*

> *A thud as WONG SIEN pushes over a chair, he throws a package out from under it. FOON SING joins him. DORIS watches the two as they retrieve packages from the chairs pushing over each chair with a thud as they do so. As they work ROBERT goes to the drinks table and pours a drink. He takes it to DORIS. She smiles as she takes it. ROBERT joins WONG SIEN and FOON SING. Lights are changing.*

> *The three men will push over the chairs tossing out the packages. They work efficiently, not rushed but quickly, thuds punctuating their work. The packages will be packed into the suitcase. Once all the packages are collected the men will pile the red bound chairs one on top of another into a rough pyramid-like structure to one side of the periphery.*

> *DORIS drinks her drink as she watches the men. FOON SING finishes piling the red bound chairs up as ROBERT passes the suitcase to WONG SIEN.*

ROBERT
> Done.

WONG SIEN
> Not quite.

> *FOON SING begins a move to leave the area. The fragmented piano music has become one repeated note.*

Stop. *(FOON SING stops.)* Are you a man of your word? *(FOON SING nods his head.)* Then you will do what is necessary.

FOON SING
Is it necessary?

WONG SIEN
If you value your own life, it is necessary.

FOON SING looks towards JANET.

WONG SIEN
(to ROBERT) I trust you will see to it.

ROBERT gives a small nod of the head. WONG SIEN shakes his hand and exits with the suitcase between the walls. ROBERT turns to look at DORIS. She kisses his cheek and exits between the walls. He looks to FOON SING. The piano stops. Neither speaks. After a moment ROBERT moves towards the bar, casually picking up the gun and pocketing it on the way to the bar. He will pour two drinks at the bar.

ROBERT
How long has it been, Willie?

FOON SING
How long?

ROBERT
Mmmn, since you've been with us, how long?

JANET opens her eyes. She looks straight ahead, not at the men.

FOON SING
Fourteen years old come to Canada. Golden mountain. First work in laundry in Moose Jaw.

ROBERT
And then?

FOON SING
And then you know.

ROBERT
But tell me.

FOON SING
Wong Sien save me in Moose Jaw and bring me to you. Life is better.

ROBERT
Yes, life is better. *(FOON SING nods in agreement.)* I've been good to you, eh? And Doris too? Eh?

FOON SING
Yes, good. *(taking the drink ROBERT offers)*

ROBERT
Drink to that, shall we?

FOON SING joins him, a silent toast. They drink. ROBERT motions for FOON SING to sit in the other wingback. He sits.

I like you Willie. Wong Sien is right. I know I can rely on you. And you know you can rely on me. We both know what happens when reliance and trust fail… *(He sits on the arm of the wingback in which JANET is sitting.)* I had a horse once. Beautiful animal. A jumper. I don't know what happened. What went wrong. It started to balk. To come up short. The thing was…. It got something into its head, a gear went click and it just stopped…. Stopped – listening. It seemed to forget which was the horse and which was the rider. *(He gets up.)* One day I'd had enough. I shot the damn thing, and I don't regret it.

Pause.

Still.

I often think of that horse. When I find myself in a sticky situation? When a red flag goes up, and a decision has to be made – I think to myself, well Robert, you've got a choice. You can ride, or be ridden… *(He takes out the gun.)* and it never takes too long to come up with an answer. When it's you or the horse, the answer's easy to come by.

FOON SING goes to the bar, and puts his drink down. Pause. A low almost subliminal and slow baa-boom, creeps in at intervals under the following:

Do you want me to do it?

Pause. FOON SING goes to ROBERT who hands him the gun. ROBERT finishes his drink, goes to the table, and puts his glass down. FOON SING points the gun at ROBERT. ROBERT turns from the bar to FOON SING. ROBERT, while aware of the threat, is undisturbed by it. His following statement is simply business, not an attempt to appease FOON SING.

ROBERT
Everything will be covered. Looked after. You know that, don't you.

FOON SING cocks the gun, an audible click. A brief pause, then ROBERT turns and leaves as FOON SING tracks his movement with the gun. ROBERT stops and turns back to look at FOON SING.

ROBERT
> Good night Willie.

> *He exits between the walls. After a moment FOON SING uncocks the gun and lowers it.*

JANET
> I can read minds, Willie.
> I can read your mind.
> It's alright.
> This is what we'll do. (*She stands up gathering up the sheet in her arms as she does so. She moves away from the chair.*) Promise me…. You promise…. Promise. You will go into the kitchen, and peel the potatoes.
> I will go into the basement, and iron the laundry.
> I'll take the gun from the drawer in the hallway.
> The iron is hot… the basement is cool…
> In the kitchen, you'll hear it.

> (*pause*) You'll find me.

> (*pause*) It won't be over.

> (*pause*) Foon Sing?

> *She raises her arms, as the sheet flutters out like a cape or wings behind her.*

<u>I love you!</u>

> *An extremely loud resonant sound accompanied by a blinding flash. In that flash we see JANET collapse to the floor the sheet billowing around her and down covering her body as FOON SING drops the gun. He kneels beside JANET. Their position is reminiscent of that at the end of Act One.*

> *A momentary suspension in time.*

> *There is the sound of blood moving through chambers, through channels and the faint drum of a heartbeat. An acrid smell of gunpowder is in the air.*

FOON SING
> I did not want this. I do care for you. (*He touches her face.*) Did you have feelings for me?

> *A moment later all sound stops. Blackout.*

> *The end.*

Angel's Trumpet

PLAYWRIGHT'S NOTES

In *Angel's Trumpet* the turbulent relationship between Scott and Zelda Fitzgerald is encapsulated in a meeting with Zelda's psychiatrist. Scott, on the verge of breakdown himself, demands a diagnosis of Zelda's literary ambitions as evidence of her escalating mental deterioration. While the psychiatrist attempts to mediate, the couple squares off against each other using as their weapons the events of their past, present, and eventually their projected future. The struggle between these two passionate and talented individuals is underscored by the tapping of a typewriter's keys as a stenographer documents the meeting.

Angel's Trumpet is what I make from the lives of Scott, once described as the foremost literary talent of his time, and his wife, Zelda. What interests me is the nature of the ownership of a life and its transformation into a literary (or dramatic) text, and whether one individual's urge for self-expression can be justifiably sacrificed if it's deemed necessary for the self-expression of a genius (as some described Scott Fitzgerald). Perhaps more important for me is the question, where does the truth lie? In the living of our lives, or in the multiple ways and means we have of recording them? Of course in the end the only thing that really interests me is the complex and compelling relationship between two talented and passionate people locked in a struggle born out of love, hate and circumstance, and from which it seems neither can emerge victorious.

Angel's Trumpet was first produced by Theatre Junction, Calgary, Alberta, in February 2001, with the following company:

Dr. Michael Renton	Daniel Arnold
Zelda Sayre Fitzgerald	Maev Beatty
Miss Laheursa	Shawna Burnett
Francis Key Scott Fitzgerald	Trevor Leigh

Artistic Director: Mark Lawes
Directed by Sharon Pollock
Set/Lighting Designed by Terry Gunvordahl
Costumes Designed by Deneen McArthur
Props Designed by Kate Lawes
Stage Managed by Robina Cook

The playwright wishes to thank:
Artistic Director Mark Lawes and the Theatre Junction Acting and Production Ensemble for their on-going commitment to her work;
Don Peacock for providing access to his extensive library of books by and about the Fitzgeralds;
The Canada Council for the Arts for its support through the playwright-in-residence program;
Alberta Playwrights' Network for its workshop services.

CHARACTERS

ZELDA SAYRE FITZGERALD	a woman of 33 years
FRANCIS KEY SCOTT FITZGERALD	a man of 36 years
DR. MICHAEL RENTON	a psychiatrist, early 30's
MISS LAHEURSA	an older woman who, as the stenographer, transcribes and records the meeting

PLACE

La Paix, ZELDA and SCOTT Fitzgerald's home outside of Baltimore; eleven months after ZELDA's release from the Phipps Psychiatric Clinic; seven months after the publication of her novel *Save Me the Waltz*; nine months prior to her recommitment to Phipps Psychiatric Clinic and the serial publication of *Tender is the Night* by SCOTT Fitzgerald.

SETTING

Set and set pieces as dictated by a particular production's concept. Required are: Two armchairs in close proximity to a coffee table; beside one chair is RENTON's briefcase containing notebook, pen, and ZELDA's case file;
A bar with liquor, primarily gin, no mix, and glasses;
A minimalist sculpture a portion of which (or the sculpture itself depending on size) lies on the floor as if thrown there. It has a skeletal appearance like a fragment of skull and looks as if it's been exposed to extreme heat. Beneath it is a red slipper;
A straight-backed chair that has been brought into this room from another room, probably the dining room;
A pouf or art deco style small bench suitable for sitting on;
A chair and small table or desk on which sits a pile of paper and a machine for the transcribing or recording of the meeting. The machine is practical and similar, or identical, to that used by a court reporter in the 30s. The sound of the keys when hit is soft, muted, just barely audible. LAHEURSA uses shorthand to record the meeting. It is not necessary for her to strike a key for every letter of every word spoken.

NOTES

The sound as LAHEURSA transcribes and records the meeting provides an aural counterpoint to, and comment on, the spoken words, as well as on their transformation from spoken to written with attendant interpretive variance. The sound always lags a couple of seconds behind the spoken words. The cue for characters is the spoken word and not the sound of a key striking paper. That sound is absent (except for the lag) during "pause" or "silence." It is important that the sound of the keys and the absence of that sound be carefully orchestrated.
SCOTT ignores LAHEURSA's physical presence even when referring to her, until the end of the play.

Angel's Trumpet
— — • — — • — —

Sound of the opening bars of "The Dance of the Wooden Soldiers." The fragment of music is slightly distorted and repeated, at first very loud, then growing fainter with each repeat.

A still picture: light revealing LAHEURSA with her back to the audience. She is wearing a black cloak and hat. She is looking at ZELDA who is not near her.

Seen less clearly, and in silhouette, are ZELDA, SCOTT, and Dr. RENTON. ZELDA is isolated, her back to LAHEURSA and the audience, her head turned, looking towards SCOTT. She is dressed in shades of red to pink, and holds a red slipper in her hand.

SCOTT and RENTON's focus is on each other. RENTON holds the straight-backed chair. SCOTT has a cigarette in one hand; the other hand is partially in his pocket, about to withdraw a lighter. They are in a soft freeze until SCOTT speaks.

LAHEURSA
Zelda.

ZELDA turns her gaze from SCOTT to LAHEURSA. LAHEURSA steps aside to reveal the broken piece of sculpture on the floor. ZELDA moves to it, kneels down, and picks it up.

SCOTT
Now. *(a flame flares from his lighter)* To begin

He lights his cigarette. He picks up his drink from the coffee table. "The Dance of the Wooden Soldiers" is cross fading with faint sound of wind and flames.

The following action and dialogue (indicated as [A] and [B] in the script) happen simultaneously. LAHEURSA and ZELDA might be thought of as sharing one reality, with SCOTT and RENTON sharing a second and separate reality. Each couple has not acknowledged and does not acknowledge the other couple until [X] is indicated in the script.

[A] LAHEURSA moves to the small desk. ZELDA stands; she carries the pair of red slippers and returns the sculpture fragment to its original place in the room. She remains by the sculpture her focus on her hand as it rests on the sculpture. LAHEURSA takes off her cloak and hat, placing her cloak— revealing its red lining—on the back of the chair and her hat on the desk. Her somewhat ominous appearance is reduced to that of a rather dowdy older stenographer. She sits in the chair, rolls a sheet of paper into the

machine, ready to document the meeting. This sheet of paper will not be replaced or removed from the machine till the end of the play. [A]

[B]:

SCOTT
I think I'd like the chair... there.

He indicates a position of isolation, nowhere near the coffee table and its armchairs. RENTON, after a moment of consideration, places the chair at the coffee table making a threesome of chairs.

No.

RENTON
I don't think–

SCOTT
I said there.

RENTON, refusing to comply with SCOTT's request, steps away from the straight-backed chair.

I want the chair *(butting out his cigarette, putting down his drink, places the chair isolated centre stage, its back to the audience)* There! Now.... To begin– *(picks up his glass and takes a drink)* [B]

[X] The two realities have merged. LAHEURSA begins her transcribing of the meeting with SCOTT's next word.

Zelda.

Sound of wind and flame out. ZELDA looks at him.

Sit.

She sits in one of the armchairs. He indicates the straight-backed chair.

Sit!

ZELDA smiles at SCOTT, gets up, moves to the straight-backed chair, sits, her back to the audience, and puts on her slippers. SCOTT downs his drink, turns to pour another. ZELDA and RENTON watch him but quickly avert their gaze, as he looks to them. SCOTT almost catches their observation of him. He suspects it.

What is it?

ZELDA looks at SCOTT and smiles. RENTON busies himself removing a notebook, pen, and ZELDA's case file from his briefcase. He will sit in one of the armchairs.

What?... What's she smiling at?

RENTON
I don't know.

SCOTT
You don't know?

RENTON
Perhaps she finds something funny.

SCOTT
Funny?

RENTON
Or – Odd.

SCOTT
She finds something odd?

RENTON
Perhaps.

SCOTT
Perhaps?... You know I know what's going on between you two. I know it.

RENTON
What's going on? *(pause)*

SCOTT
Nothing. *(pause)* I'm sorry. I'm... tired. *(gives a small cough)* Things get... away on me. *(He takes a drink.)* This cough, for one thing. Incipient TB.

RENTON
Really.

SCOTT
Yes really. Isn't it in her case file? Don't you read her case file? My incipient TB? Lost me one year at Princeton, you didn't read that?

RENTON
It was more of a rhetorical "really."

SCOTT
Really? *(pause)* Is she taking this down?

RENTON
Isn't that what you asked for? Everything recorded?

SCOTT
Yes, from beginning to end. Have we begun?

RENTON
What use is it?

SCOTT
Is what?

RENTON
The transcription, the record, it has no legal standing.

SCOTT
It may…. Or may not. It has standing with Zelda and me. The words. Material. Concrete. Captured. Not ephemeral. Eternal. Enduring. I endure. I endure, Zelda!

And she knows what I want from this meeting! She knows exactly what I want and I know that she knows it!

Pause. After a moment RENTON begins to tap his pen on the coffee table.

Would you stop that! *(snatching the pen from RENTON and placing it on the coffee table)* Thank you. *(pause)*

Well, are you going to sit there like patience on a monument or are we going to begin?

RENTON
What do you want me to do?

SCOTT
Your job.

RENTON
My job? I don't approve of any of this. You went over my head so I'm here. To – mediate. To witness – whatever, I'm not sure what. I won't be party to the forcing of things.

SCOTT
Won't you? Are you pretending for her? Pretending you're unaware that the forcing of things is precisely what you are here for? What the institution you work for is dedicated to!

RENTON
A somewhat twisted view of psychiatry.

SCOTT

I–! *(pause)* Apologize! I take back those words. They're not what I meant. I have… I have the greatest faith in– *(pause)* It's obvious. I mean *(pause)* I must have, otherwise– *(pause)* Otherwise. *(He takes a drink.)*

Faith.

RENTON

In psychiatry?

SCOTT

No. Nothing. I'm rambling, ignore what I said, just – Ignore it.

RENTON

You requested I be here. So I'm here. To give, I suppose, this discussion some formal standing. What I'm saying, for the record, is that I quarrel with the forcing of things.

SCOTT

The two of us could quarrel about a number of things. I'm tired of quarrelling. What I am is bankrupt. Physically and mentally bankrupt. Soon to be financially bankrupt if things are not resolved. And now? Now I am directing all of my energies to the most difficult task of trying to think straight. To plot a path – to say nothing of a novel.

Do you understand what I'm talking about? Do you understand that the fate of this family is borne on my back? On my back! *(pause)* I doubt you understand that.

(He pours himself another drink.) Yes I'm having a drink. I am having Another Drink. Is there a look exchanged between the two of you behind my back? I…. Wonder.

(He turns back to RENTON.) Let me be frank with you Doctor. I suspect – more than suspect – I sit this far from knowing – you have been seduced, charmed, and taken in by this woman who is adept at seducing and charming, when she wants to be.

(cuts off RENTON's attempted response) When She Wants to Be. Or is able. She is not always Able. These seductive talents she does not expend on me. And while her treasure chest of such talents is depleted, it is not yet empty. You have bought into her version of our relationship. Why? Because she has charmed you in her lucid moments. Don't deny it! And I suspect – more than suspect – know, know that you are moving, have moved, from analysis and treatment of Zelda to certain observations and presumptions concerning myself.

RENTON

I look at the patient in the context of her environment. That's all it amounts to.

SCOTT
For example! A question that rattles round in your head is, did my drinking drive Zelda to Bedlam, or did a crazy Zelda drive me to drink? My answer? Who cares! For that is a simple question not worth one minute's consideration when so much larger things are at stake. My work, for one thing. My art. Yes I presume to say that. My Art. And the survival of my child, myself, and my wife.

RENTON
So are we here to form some definitive statement regarding your drinking

RENTON
(simultaneously with SCOTT) is that what we're here for?

SCOTT
(simultaneously with RENTON) That's got nothing to do with it!

SCOTT
I asked – No! Not asked. Demanded! Demanded this meeting to resolve one question. One question only. If the functioning member of this family is to continue functioning, how do we bring that about and what is presently preventing it?

> Slight pause.

Is that two questions?

(Just as RENTON attempts an answer, SCOTT continues.) Suppose it is, what does it matter? I've asked for that resolution to be transcribed, documented and agreed to by her, by you, and by me. It's as simple as that. No one'll wriggle round the "he said I said you said" this time. It will Be There, on Paper.

See, Zelda, see!... You see her?... That is a stenographer, Zelda, a recorder who has come with the doctor! At my request!... Yes?

> ZELDA gets up and drifts past SCOTT to look at LAHEURSA. SCOTT turns back to RENTON.

Now – I trust your education and profession enable you to deduce which is the functioning member of the Fitzgerald menage.... Well go on, speak!

> During the following ZELDA unobtrusively moves about the room sometimes seeming oblivious to the dialogue but she is taking in more than it seems.

RENTON
I said I'm here to help.

SCOTT
Slight change from "mediate."

RENTON
If you feel a transcription helpful you'll have it. And if you had concerns regarding any perceived bias on my part, you could've approached me directly.

SCOTT
I know Gebhardt better.

RENTON
Our relationship is not an adversarial one, Mr. Fitzgerald

SCOTT
Scott.

RENTON
Scott.

SCOTT
Then why do I feel that it is?

RENTON
I've no idea.

SCOTT
Not reassuring. I thought the inner workings of the mind were your specialty. I thought that's what I paid you for. And yet you have no idea regarding the nature of our relationship and cannot name the functioning member of my family. Are you similarly devoid of ideas when it comes to my wife's treatment?

RENTON
It seems you feel things have not been going well.

SCOTT
Bloody brilliant. *(moving to get another drink)*

RENTON
Do you think that's wise?

SCOTT
I think it's necessary. Would you like one?

RENTON
No thanks.

SCOTT
I didn't think so. I'm forced to drink alone.

He turns to find ZELDA sitting in the armchair he has just vacated to get his drink.

I don't apologize. It's an amenity of life of which I have few. *(brief pause)* Actually – I thought I might offer a congratulatory toast but it would be – Premature, I take it?

RENTON
Who told you?

SCOTT
Dr. Gebhardt again. He whispers your – promotion to a Clinic partnership is imminent. Those in charge of such momentous decisions are impressed with your diagnostic talent and treatment skills. Apparently.

RENTON
That's good to know.

SCOTT
At least I think that's what he said.

RENTON
Your congratulations are accepted.

SCOTT
Though it's still not "in the bag," so to speak.

RENTON
As good as.

ZELDA *picks up her case file from the coffee table.*

SCOTT
Yes. Well. *(He takes the case file from her.)* Life deals many unexpected blows. And you have no idea.

RENTON
About what?

SCOTT
The source of my concern regarding our relationship, yours and mine!

RENTON
In these cases–

SCOTT
You have many cases like my wife's?

ZELDA *gets up from the armchair.*

RENTON
Well no but–

SCOTT
I'm an expert. I know her case intimately. I've lived with it for three years and her forever. It has circumscribed and defined my life and work. "In these cases" – Go on!

ZELDA resumes her perambulation round the room, and will eventually chose to sit on the pouf or bench, with her back to SCOTT and RENTON.

RENTON
A degree of neutrality–

SCOTT
I disagree.

RENTON
Objectivity might be a better word.

SCOTT
It might. Or it might not. Are you familiar with "he who pays the piper calls the tune?"

RENTON
Well, in a psychiatric case the welfare of the patient–

SCOTT
I know the patient and her history best. My mind is clear. Hers is not. I've always played a role in Zelda's treatment. I've worked with doctors to determine what's best for Zelda. Since you took over my role has been reduced. I'm not consulted as I once was nor as I wish to be. Do you think this has any bearing on my sense of our relationship?

RENTON
Zelda's best interests–

SCOTT
Why've you sent me no bills lately? No outpatient bills for Zelda's sessions? I get the Clinic's bills, but none from you.

RENTON
I'm an admirer of your work and talent, Mr. Fitz–

SCOTT
Scott.

RENTON
Scott.

SCOTT
And?

RENTON

And I'm aware of your financial position.

SCOTT

Bullshit! – As Ernest would say. We Princeton men would simply smile
politely and change the subject. Perhaps Zelda needs to move on. A new
doctor perhaps. Or better still, back. To a previous doctor, one who sees her
particular case more clearly. To Gebhardt perhaps.

RENTON

It's up to you.

SCOTT

Yes it is.

RENTON

So whatever you want.

SCOTT

Would such a request blot your record of achievement at the Phipps Clinic?

RENTON

I can forward a bill if you want. Whatever you prefer.

SCOTT

I prefer nothing. I carry on carry on carry on carry carry on… carry on. *(pause)*
Have I made myself clear?

RENTON

To a degree. However–

SCOTT

How. Ever. What.

RENTON

However…. Let's go on.

SCOTT

By all means. Go on. You do know she knows all this, don't you?

RENTON

Knows what?

SCOTT

What is at stake here! She knows it. And she tells you more than she knows
about other things too, and you believe her.

RENTON

What things?

SCOTT
My drinking. Her writing.

RENTON
She talks, I listen.

SCOTT
She lies! She's always been reckless and bold. Beautiful once. With not one scintilla of insecurity or trace of moral principle when I met her. Boodling with the boys. A drunk at seventeen. My mistress a year before marriage, and me not one of the first.

Notorious in two states and a range of southern colleges. All with her mother's connivance and any consequence of her actions blocked by her father's name and position. It began there. Not with me. There!

 Pause.

Is she putting this in? *(a reference to the transcript)*

RENTON
She is.

SCOTT
A Review of her History. That's got to be there. *(RENTON indicates for SCOTT to go on.)* Committed for fifteen months to Prangins Clinic in Switzerland. Why? Because she's literally dancing herself to death, trying at age twenty-nine to turn into Pavlova. A demented and competitive desire to pit herself in dance against me and my words in print!

Not my assessment, theirs.

RENTON
But – you disagree?

SCOTT
I agree! They hit it bang on. She's released, with certain stipulations as to what she can and cannot do in the interests of her health. Dancing she cannot do. We return home. Five months later in a hyperactive state, she's committed to Phipps. This time driven by a berserk determination to beat me at my own game in the literary field. A clear re-emergence of her competitive compulsion first diagnosed at Prangins. Do you agree?

RENTON
I'm listening.

SCOTT
You're listening. But then you know all this don't you.

RENTON
She's been my patient for a number of months.

SCOTT
Then why don't we move on to her novel fiasco? For which I hold the Clinic and you you personally responsible! Her novel. Which places in jeopardy not only the marketing of my own novel but also the viability of my future work upon which our livelihood depends! She's released, with certain activities prohibited, and now it all begins again!

I'll give you my diagnosis in a nutshell doctor. She sees her salvation in my destruction, and is incapable of comprehending that my destruction brings about her destruction! Now do you understand what I'm saying?

RENTON
I understand what you've said. I'm not sure I understand what you're saying.

SCOTT
I've tried very hard to like you Dr. Renton. I'm trying very hard to believe that we're working together on Zelda's behalf, and for the ultimate good of Zelda, my daughter and myself.

RENTON
Zelda's my patient and I'm her psychiatrist. Naturally I think of her first.

SCOTT
That may be natural. It is not reasonable! Think of my work and the family first, the impact of her actions on that. I'm Zelda's husband who is paying the bills and who is supporting her and who she is at present undermining on every front.

RENTON
In what way?

SCOTT
In – what – way. Is not her wellness totally dependent on a strict regime of approved activity and rest as determined and prescribed prior to her release from Phipps?

RENTON
That's right.

SCOTT
She clearly understood and accepted that I was to oversee her adherence to that regime?

RENTON
True.

SCOTT
Of course it's true! That's how it was! At first she complied.

RENTON
And was doing well. Is doing well.

SCOTT
Was it a true compliance?

RENTON
I thought so.

SCOTT
Or one brought about by fear?

RENTON
Fear of what?

SCOTT
Of being forcibly returned to the Clinic if she did not comply!

RENTON
I don't make threats to patients.

SCOTT
Seven months have passed, and so has that fear, be it from threats or otherwise. I'm left with an increasingly recalcitrant psychopathic personality!

RENTON
She's hardly that.

SCOTT
Are you listening to me? She is obstinately defiant of my authority. She's indulging in work, competitive work, which will lead to another mental and physical collapse, one that I in my present state am unable to tolerate financially, physically or mentally!

RENTON
What's she doing?

SCOTT
What do you mean what's she doing? She's doing what was *pro*scribed; she's not doing what was *pre*scribed! And I must be able to order her back to the institution if she continues this violation and know that you will back me up and sign her recommitment papers!

And she must be made to understand that that is her position! That she is alone! That you are not "on her side!" That she is utterly dependent on me, as is the case, and that my support of her is not without limits! And I, have reached, my limit.

RENTON
I see.

SCOTT
Do you?

RENTON
And what does Zelda say?

SCOTT
She says nothing. Smiles at nothing. Locks her room. When she's in it. When she leaves it. Disagrees incessantly or else withdraws. Talks nonsense. Is secretive and driven. And I... I am...... deep in my first novel since *Gatsby* almost six years since *Gatsby*!

RENTON
Closer to eight... I believe. *(pause)*

SCOTT
Closer... to... eight...

RENTON
Yes. Almost a decade.

SCOTT
Your point being?

RENTON
No point really, just – clarification.

SCOTT
Almost a decade as America's highest paid writer of short stories! Clear enough?

RENTON
I wasn't suggesting–

SCOTT
Deep I said! Deep in my first novel since *Gatsby*, almost eight years since *Gatsby*. I was about to say do you understand what hangs in the balance here?

RENTON
I think so.

SCOTT
And – my health – is not the best... I know that. But, I don't suppose it means a thing to either of you.... To anyone really. *(He finishes his drink. Pause.)*

RENTON

Would you like to continue this tomorrow?

SCOTT

See? I hear it. In your voice, I hear it.

RENTON

Hear what?

SCOTT

I am not your patient!

RENTON

No treatment intended. Concern expressed.

SCOTT

We will not continue this tomorrow. There are issues to be resolved; they will be resolved today.

RENTON

Alright.

SCOTT

All. Right. When will that be? When all is right... when will it be?

RENTON

You know you sound tired. Are you sure tomorrow wouldn't be better?

SCOTT

Yes, I am tired! No, tomorrow would not be better! Let me tell you something. At one time, at one time the question for me was how to save Zelda. Now, now the question is how do I save myself?

RENTON

From what?

SCOTT

From Zelda. *(pause)* Because... you see, if... if the ultimate price to be paid for my survival, is her sanity... then that is the price that must be paid. And you... you must understand that my daughter's future, my own future – even Zelda's, in whatever capacity she is able to live it, depends on, accepting the... possibility... that that, may be the ultimate price. Can you, are you able, to understand what I'm saying?

RENTON

I think, with the aid of a great deal of gin, you've extrapolated a very dark scenario from Zelda's testing the boundaries of what she can and cannot do. That's not unusual, and we can fix it.

SCOTT
You, are a very young man.

RENTON
Four years between us.

SCOTT
Do you think so?

RENTON
Four years.

SCOTT
In years. Four years between us? That may be so.

RENTON
It is so.

SCOTT
You've a mind for numbers, if not for people.

> *SCOTT sits. He closes his eyes. After a moment he opens them.*

Is she getting all this? *(referring to the stenographer)*

RENTON
I believe so.

SCOTT
(closes his eyes, then after a moment) Is it relevant?

RENTON
To what?

SCOTT
Relevant – to what. *(pause)* I don't know. *(He opens his eyes.)* To what? *(silence)* I don't know. *(pause)* I'll know when I see it. *(He gets up.)* In print.

> *He takes a drink and smiles at RENTON, with effort a successful Princeton man for a moment.*

My novel, the new one. In print the beginning of next year. I'll be finished by then. *Tender is the Night.* What do you think?

RENTON
An evocative title.

SCOTT

Yes, I think so too. Zelda's... suggestion... *(His last word fades away. He takes a drink as the Princeton man fades away.)* So.... Now...... now...

RENTON

Now we begin?

SCOTT

Begin?

RENTON

If you want.

SCOTT

I thought we had.

RENTON

Did you?

SCOTT

Well we've "gone on" haven't we, how do you go on if you haven't begun?

RENTON

Shall we go on then?

SCOTT

No, we shall not "go on!" We shall begin! At the beginning! Again!

RENTON

Just a place to start.

SCOTT

"From," to start "from!" So... so – when was it, the beginning? I've gone over it so often now I've forgotten.

RENTON

It's frustrating I know but–

SCOTT

Shut... Up. *(brief pause)*

RENTON

–but it gives Zelda a sense of the evolution of things, a trajectory from the past into the present, and possible future.

SCOTT

What?

RENTON
It gives Zelda a—

SCOTT
I heard you…. You're an amusing fellow, did you know that?

RENTON
I've said something funny?

SCOTT
Not in the least. Just the usual blather and bilge. Zelda? And Trajectory? But that hints of flight and – propulsion, doesn't it? Going Up though, not Down. Not Down! *(pause)*

At best – curving round…. Tra-jectory. *(pause)*

It's the "J" after the vowel that gives it that push I suppose. The "J," and the "C" and the "T." Traaa-jectory.

RENTON
If it helps.

SCOTT
Helps? "If it helps." Nothing helps. Once more into the breach.

The beginning. Shall we go back to Zelda hanging off her mother's teat till the year she was three? Spoilt rotten by

ZELDA
You

SCOTT
What?

ZELDA
You

SCOTT
Yes me, what about me?

ZELDA
You used a small gentleman's cane at the age of seven.

SCOTT
Her. Spoilt rotten by her mother Minnie—

ZELDA
Who did you think you were?

SCOTT
By her mother Minnie! Her father Judge Sayre, and the whole wretched family who now blame me for her condition.

ZELDA begins gently and slowly stroking her cheek.

I drove her crazy. They say that. They do. I drove her crazy, yet they're the ones taught her complete self-indulgence and not one iota of responsibility.

ZELDA
Whose diagnosis is that?

SCOTT
Breaking your code of silence uh? Don't pick at your face.

ZELDA
I'm not.

SCOTT
You have eczema. It came on at the Swiss clinic. Don't you remember?

ZELDA
I Had eczema. I don't have eczema now, not now.

SCOTT
Not at the moment, no, so don't pick at your face!

ZELDA
I'm not.

SCOTT
So what're you doing?!

ZELDA
I'm feeling my face.

SCOTT
Well don't! *(to RENTON)* You see what I'm up against? *(to ZELDA)* Stop it! Once you had skin like peaches and cream and your hair was thick like golden honey – that's all gone now! It's over!

ZELDA
Is it?

SCOTT
Yes! It's over!

And it's come to this.

ZELDA

You said I had eyes like a Southern Barbarian princess. I was in Montgomery boodling and you were in New York at that ad agency and you wrote that you finally understood why the princess was kept in the tower. And now, so do I.

SCOTT

It was me who was mad then. In love with the idea of you. *(to RENTON)* The idea of Her. Of Zelda.

ZELDA

Do I appear mad to you, doctor?

SCOTT

I admit it! I loved her courage, the supreme self-confidence and untutored defiant intelligence. I loved the absence of any feeling of inferiority, the lack of self-doubt or regret, I loved the sincerity and the selfishness. Utterly selfish. I loved the flawless skin, the savage eyes, and the burnished hair, I loved the covetous glances, I loved knowing what others sought, I had.

ZELDA

Me.

SCOTT

Yes you.

ZELDA

He thought he could wear me like a rose.

SCOTT

You were happy enough to be worn.

ZELDA

I played the role well when it suited.

SCOTT

What did I tell you? Now she admits it.

ZELDA

Admits what?

SCOTT

Deception! You deceived me! You never loved me! You loved the uniform in the beginning, then the Princeton man inside it. You caught the scent of another world, the possibility of New York and foreign fields, escape from a dreary town and a larger audience for your escapades.

ZELDA

I don't see how distortion justifies locking me up.

SCOTT

My literary ambitions, yes you loved that. Still "ambitions" were not enough.
She threw me over you know. Looked for bigger fish to fry, or reel in. Drove
me mad with her letters. Fraternity boys and football players. Until *This Side
of Paradise* was published. My "Ambition" became "Achievement." It seemed
I had a future after all. And so did she.

ZELDA

Are you saying you never loved me? *(pause)* Is that what you're trying to say?
Denying, like Peter?

SCOTT

I'd say that "denying like Peter" is a bit of a leap, what would you say, doctor?

ZELDA

He sent me pills. I thought I was pregnant and he sent me pills. I didn't take
them. It seemed somehow dishonest.

SCOTT

What would you say?

ZELDA

To take them would've been to say I didn't have the right to do what I'd done.
And I did.

SCOTT

It may not qualify as religious mania but we've been there before, mark my
words, her words, three words, "denying-like-Peter."

ZELDA

Didn't I have the right to decide to sleep with him? To love him? And I had the
right to decide not to take the pills that he sent. I gave myself the right to give
myself to him. It turned out in the end. I knew it would. I wasn't pregnant. He
was afraid. I was never afraid. Not then. And now he can't even say if he loved
me.

SCOTT

I loved you when you were carrying Scotty. When somebody asked who's your
fat friend, I loved you then.

ZELDA

I have been loved. People have loved me…. When they found me most lovable,
I was pretending. It was not really me…. Beginnings?… When I was a child
I was… always running. Is that what you want to hear? People in Montgomery
said they never saw me stand still. Run with my dog, swing from the tree by
the window, jump from high places, dive in deep water, race on my roller
skates I liked, Climbing…. On buildings under construction, scaling tall trees,
measuring steps along the apex of house roofs, shortening my skirts by rolling
the waistband! Enough?…

Parents?

Me tramping on train tracks along with my father, finding and moulding little pieces of clay. Called him "old dick" behind his back and he called me "baby" and will call me "baby" till the day that he dies! They said I was elusive and willful and my mother named me after a gypsy queen in a novel! Enough?!

How about him? He told me he was bossy and a bully at school, thought he was a prince and suspected he was really a pauper and that's why he carried a cane! The great author!

SCOTT
Began at the age of ten, published at thirteen, dedicated to writing all of my life!

ZELDA
Dedicated to drink.

SCOTT
Accusation, see, now it starts.

ZELDA
The great drunk!

SCOTT
What did I tell you?

ZELDA
And performing even for those he didn't know and cared nothing about, on all fours at the door singing "Dog! Dog! Dog!" like a dog looking for some bone of attention or admiration or adoration or altercation or anything so long as he held centre stage!

SCOTT
The location you craved!

RENTON
Shall we just

SCOTT
I couldn't sit down to write for fear of her leaving the house improvising some crazy prank!

RENTON
(*simultaneously with ZELDA*) Shall we–

ZELDA
(*simultaneously with RENTON*) What house?

Did we ever have a house? We flew from hotel rooms to apartments to rented premises on paper wings of eviction notices for drunk and unruly behaviour!

RENTON
(simultaneously with ZELDA) Can we

ZELDA
(simultaneously with RENTON) We never had a house!

We've never had a home! There's nothing solid under our feet and you marvel that my mind takes flight to the heavens?

SCOTT
What would you've done with a house? *(to RENTON)* She thought the shoemaker's elves did laundry as well as shoes, and she threw all our dirty clothes in a closet. Ceiling high in a closet! You want to try opening that door when your head pounds! and the bank's called! and her hand is out for a fox fur! and there's too many parties we can't miss and

ZELDA
you're in a rage because of a kiss!

SCOTT
the damn car's on the fritz again

ZELDA
we're up for an interview times ten!

SCOTT
Scribners' late with a small advance

ZELDA
you can't find a jacket to match your pants?

SCOTT
the literary hacks are hoping I fail

ZELDA
and the eviction notice?

SCOTT
has come in the mail!

ZELDA and SCOTT laugh. Pause and silence.

ZELDA
But you wrote. Marvelous stories.

SCOTT
Short ones. Short. Stories. Buying time for the novels to come

ZELDA
and money for jam.

SCOTT
Novels to come

ZELDA
and "Gloria" threaded through "Zelda" threaded through me.

SCOTT
As it turns out

ZELDA
Threaded through with a needle.

SCOTT
aborting novels to come. *(pause)*

ZELDA
My room was always thick with the fragrance of pears…. Sometimes I would slice off a piece and send it to you in a letter.

SCOTT
I love you. You know that. *(to RENTON)* She knows it.

ZELDA
(to SCOTT) But it's not about love, is it? *(to RENTON)* He tries to get into my room, and I'm asking you not to let him destroy my work.

SCOTT
Darling darling, listen to me. I am at your door. I am trying to get in. The reason being, when you lock yourself in none of us in the house can rest easy.

ZELDA
I'm working in there.

SCOTT
Working on what, Zelda? On what? *(to RENTON)* Ask her on what.

ZELDA
I'm a disciplined person. I like to do things.

SCOTT
And the schedule is simple. Just join Scotty and me at table three times a day. In the morning tennis, swimming, or riding – just, some form of exercise. Then lunch. Then – Why can't you spend some time with Scotty? After all you're her

mother!… Afternoon exercise?… Some time dedicated to your painting, don't you like painting?… A medicinal bath, dinner, with free time in the evening, and to bed at ten. Is that really so difficult? Is it so unreasonable?

ZELDA

Every every every every every ever ever ever ever ever ever more!!!

SCOTT

Thank you. *(returns to the drinks table)* I believe I will have another.

ZELDA

Another drink.

SCOTT

How perceptive. You may watch.

ZELDA

He saw me at a script dance and my card was full. I danced a solo and he watched, didn't you watch?

SCOTT

(as he gets a drink) Oh yes I watched I watched.

ZELDA

Although he prefers being watched. And the pavilion was hot, and we sat on my porch swing, breathing magnolia and pear while the airmen from Taylor Field stunted in planes over my house, and asked me to marry them. Yes! I took their pins and silver bars, put them in a cigar box and said no! I boodled at Boodler's Bend drank gin and when there was no gin drank corn liquor cut with cola, kissing a man with a moustache because I never had before!

I never played for an audience. I did it all for myself and I never cared what anyone thought. They said I swam in the nude, wrote "what the hell – Zelda Sayre!" under my picture, and when the night air was heavy, took my petticoat off and gave it to one of the boys to carry, and took turns breaking Victrola records over each other's head when the party got dull. They said I danced too close and was too affectionate on the dance floor, so I pinned mistletoe on my backside and kept on dancing dancing dancing!

Ooohh, this might be important! When I was little I phoned the fire department to report a child up on a roof who couldn't get down and then I climbed up on the roof and I pushed the ladder away and I waited for the fire truck and the sirens. They came! Now what do you think?

Something was always about to happen, and if it didn't, I made it!

I knew that the edge was more interesting than the middle and the leap more so than the slide – If you're going to fall, Jump!

You told me you were a Princeton man, you were going to be famous, going to go overseas, going to die leading your men "Over the Top!" He made things like that up in his head. Going to come home and Write. Great Author. Magnificent Novels. That was his story. Each of us thought we were the major character in our own sensational tale but, we never read through to the end.

So I said yes and the war was over and he didn't go over the top he went to New York, and nobody wanted his stories and I said no because I knew it would only mean he needed to prove to himself he could still win, Something, Anything, Me! And it would be no good. He didn't really want the kind of a girl that would have him then, and I knew it.

Then he sold to *Smart Set* and Scribners and the *Saturday Evening Post* and *This Side of Paradise* and they said in his book he'd invented the flapper, "created the new American girl in rebellion" and I was proud it was me he'd caught and flung out into the world, proud I was his fictional girl, and I loved him, and I said yes because it was right then and he bought me a platinum and diamond wristwatch but later I threw it away and all the clothes I'd designed I burnt in the bathtub when he told me I did nothing and had no talent and made no effort and he was in thrall to an eighteen-year-old vapid would be Hollywood virginal vamp who was disciplined and worked hard, and I was twenty-seven years old then!

SCOTT
I never ever saw her with her mother not present, you know that!

ZELDA
So I started ballet and wrote.

SCOTT
You tell him!

ZELDA
I sold three articles that year but they put both our names on them and I didn't care

SCOTT
You betrayed me!

ZELDA
We got more money that way!

SCOTT
(to RENTON) When I was doing my best work ever!

ZELDA
But we never knew where it went!

photo: Charles Hope Photography

l to r: Maev Beatty, Daniel Arnold.

SCOTT
Betrayed at Valescure and it was never the same!

ZELDA
and he kept my letters and took their words and now only their shadows fall on the page!

SCOTT
A bond was broken!

ZELDA
And when George Jean Nathan wanted to publish my diaries you said no, you said you found them inspiring, useful in your own writing!

SCOTT
You broke it!

ZELDA
You said they belonged to you and that was in 1920 and everyone came to our place in Westport or New York or wherever we lived he would ask them and I would call them and say no no because of the baby!

SCOTT
She broke it!

ZELDA
I was trying you see! She was sleeping! and we were always drunk and being asked to leave by landlords and hosts and avoided by friends when we weren't so funny any more!

SCOTT
Her!

ZELDA
eating fresh spinach and drinking old champagne for breakfast and lunch and dinner turning cartwheels

SCOTT
Not me!

ZELDA
Cartwheels!

SCOTT
So don't you throw that young woman into the mix!

ZELDA
Cartwheels turning turning cartwheels turning!

SCOTT

That relationship was one of absolute innocence!

ZELDA

Turning cartwheels in New York hotel lobbies and playing in the fountain in Union Square and spinning round and round and round for more than half an hour in the revolving door at the Commodore spending too much money!

SCOTT

What's the use?

ZELDA

Necking with his friends because I liked their noses and turning up at parties after midnight and spending my words in apology for obnoxious behaviour Please Forgive My–! I'm So Sorry For–!! Once Again I Must–!!! *(pause)*

Pregnant... after Scotty... "it's your decision... don't you women know how to fix... that kind of – Thing?" *(pause)*

SCOTT

That was you. You decided. I left it all up to you.

ZELDA

Yes *(pause)*

RENTON

(to ZELDA) Do you regret that decision?

SCOTT

Mothering is as foreign a concept to Zelda as doing the laundry.

RENTON

(to ZELDA) Do you regret it?

SCOTT

She didn't regret it so much that she didn't return for two more. Eh Zelda? Abortions, two more abortions. And when we wanted a son, it just wouldn't take, would it Zelda? *(pause)* What would we have done with a son? *(pause)* A crazy idea.

RENTON

Zelda

ZELDA

No.... There's nothing I regret... I regret nothing.

SCOTT

Not even Jozan? *(pause)* Not even Jozan!

ZELDA

Jumbles of people and chaos and quarrels, you broke the door and bloodied my nose, my eye was black and my sister left in a cab.

SCOTT

An isolated incident years before, we were both impossibly drunk, and out of control.

ZELDA

Yes.

SCOTT

I was abjectly sorry and said so numerous times.

ZELDA

Yes.

SCOTT

Note it's a clever deflection. I ask about Jozan, she talks about eyes and a tawdry event in the past of which I am quite rightfully ashamed, Although! Although not altogether to blame.

ZELDA

Deflection?... Yes. A kind of deflection. A Misconception.

SCOTT

That Jozan loved you, and he didn't.

ZELDA

That the Riviera would be cheap and it wasn't.

SCOTT

I wasted time and talent for three years amusing and chaperoning her. Raising hell and drinking. A glut of parties and a gross of good times.

ZELDA

All for me, was it? Being force-fed your friends and their *bon mots*?

SCOTT

After *The Beautiful and the Damned* I averaged less than a hundred words a day for three years. Tell me how I recoup what was lost?

ZELDA

And you rendered "Gloria" out of my meat.

SCOTT

My most important resolution at Valescure?

ZELDA
Overcome your laziness and self-doubt?

SCOTT
To stop referring everything to you!

ZELDA
Wait till you're finished. Then – *"Revisions with Zelda."*

SCOTT
Finished, oh it was finished alright. Your grand romance with a Frenchman? You closing and leaning against the door of my workroom? Bravely confessing the love of the century? Resolutely demanding divorce? Like a bad movie, Zelda. Melodramatic and glib.

ZELDA
I was tired of parties and people and clever and smart and painting over despair with Elizabeth Arden cosmetics and that is the reason for that!

SCOTT
I should've suspected her youthful passion for airmen had surfaced when he started dipping his wings over the Villa Marie. A bit of *deja vu* there.

Your grand love affair flaunted on the casino dance floor and in the hot sand in front of the villa? While inside I laboured on the best American novel ever written. A conscious artistic endeavour!

Did she say that he loved her? He called it a mild flirtation. No grand romance there. He didn't want you my dear. Not in any permanent sense. You were just a bit of casino copulation, a fuck on a fly-by. Am I right, Zelda?

I asked for a meeting, wanted him to tell me directly, to lay out his love for my wife. Well, I had a very long wait. Monsieur Jozan was a no-show at the O.K. Corral at the Villa Marie in Valescure.

Has she told you how I locked her in a room till she came to her senses? Sometimes for a week? Sometimes for a fortnight? Maybe I did. Maybe I didn't. What does it matter?

What matters, what lasts, is the book… and what was salvaged and transformed from your dismal little affair.

ZELDA puts her hands over her ears and starts to sway slightly.

The crystallization of Gatsby, a poor bastard in love with a girl completely incapable of returning his love and commitment. Gatsby dying, as bereft of his illusions of Daisy, as I was of your allegiance to me.

He pulls her hands from her ears.

I would like you to contradict one thing that I've said, Zelda, one thing!

Pause. He releases her hands.

And you attempt to set this sordid episode of too many cocktails and sand in your panties on the same shelf as my enchantment with a young woman of exceptional talent and dedication? And to sell it to him as goods of equal value?

He turns on RENTON. ZELDA begins to hum "The March of the Wooden Soldiers."

And you, my good doctor, you buy it!

RENTON
You assume that.

SCOTT
Assume?

RENTON
Based on very little evidence, sir.

SCOTT
Sir is it? Oh it's sir now. Does the light dawn as to who is employer and who is employee?

As the dialogue continues ZELDA begins to move, a pattern of simple dance steps to her humming which will grow slowly in volume while her dance steps become increasingly complex and quicker. The men ignore her.

RENTON
My position is not that of–

SCOTT
And how is your other work coming?

RENTON
Other work? What other work?

SCOTT
Zelda tells me you too have a book in the offing.

RENTON
Not at all.

SCOTT
Or is it a play?

l to r: Trevor Leigh, Shawna Burnett, Maev Beatty, Daniel Arnold.

RENTON
No writing at all.

SCOTT
Except for your "notes?"

RENTON
Except for my notes.

ZELDA's movements and humming are becoming more and more obtrusive, louder, faster.

SCOTT
She swears the two of you discuss nothing else in your sessions. Your writing, Her writing. What do you say?

RENTON
I'd say it's her imagination at work.

SCOTT
Really?

RENTON
A projection of sorts.

SCOTT
Then you're not feeding off Zelda and me with some writing in mind?

They raise their voices to be heard above her humming which has become more of "Dum ta ta ta ta dum dum dum!" and move to avoid her when she comes near or passes between them. Her "dance" is becoming more physical as she lightly strikes herself in time with her music and movement.

RENTON
Certainly not.

SCOTT
A shocking violation of the patient doctor relationship, wouldn't you say?

RENTON
If the accusation were true.

SCOTT
And I hesitate to think what Dr. Gebhardt would say.

They must shout now to be heard above ZELDA.

RENTON
What precisely are you accusing me of?

SCOTT
I'm not accusing, I'm confiding, I'm confiding in you what she confided in me.

RENTON
You should consider the source.

SCOTT
Ah, the source. Zelda you mean. You mean the source is not to be trusted?

ZELDA is whirling round and round, her singing growing in volume; she is out of control.

Stop it!… Zelda! Stop Zelda stop!! Stop!

RENTON grabs her, enveloping her in his arms, restraining her arms at her side.

RENTON
Shhhhhh. Shhhhh. Shhhhh. Shhhh. Shhh.

RENTON's "shhhhh" continues. SCOTT watches the following: ZELDA struggles, her "song" begins to decrease in volume. RENTON, still restraining her, gently backs her into the straight-backed chair and sits her down. She gradually ceases any resistance and her "song" fades to silence. When RENTON is certain she is past this crisis he places her hands in her lap, folds them, smoothes her hair back from her face, and steps away. He adjusts his jacket. He becomes aware of SCOTT's eyes locked on him. Pause. SCOTT shifts his gaze to ZELDA in the chair, her back to the audience.

SCOTT
He says your word is not to be trusted, Zelda.

RENTON
That is not what I said.

SCOTT
Now whose side do you think he's on?

RENTON
We're not choosing sides and I believe I said a projection of sorts.

SCOTT
Meaning what?

RENTON
Meaning she may be projecting–

SCOTT
Let me guess. I'm getting good at this. She's projecting onto you something she is doing herself.

RENTON
Or wishes to do.

SCOTT
Or is doing herself. Let's examine the first premise. Zelda's Word Can Not be Trusted. In which case she is projecting onto you something she is doing herself—

RENTON
Wishes! to do.

SCOTT
Which is writing a book. She is writing a book – despite your assuring me she is not! Second premise. Zelda's Word Can be Trusted, and she says You're writing a book.

Then I say you're in deep shit my friend and acting with a grievous disregard for professional ethics. I would not bank on that partnership, doctor.

So which do you prefer? Are you writing a study of the Fitzgeralds for the masses? Or aiding Zelda in concealing the fact that she's writing a second novel?

RENTON
Have you seen any real evidence of this novel, or only imagine it?

SCOTT
Is it psychiatry's view that past experience counts for nothing?

RENTON
Everything's speculation on your part! Psychiatry's view is paranoia, exacerbated by drink!

SCOTT
That is Zelda talking! Listen to me! In Europe she was dancing eighteen hours a day, consumed with Egorova and lessons, dancing, endless and awkward in front of the gilded whore's mirror and "The March of the Wooden Soldiers" with endless irrational monologues on ballet! Sleeping with her toes hooked, and feet bent under the iron frame of our bed! Bruising from poor distended muscles on the inside of her thighs!

My marriage in pieces, Zelda going mad, and me trying to escape on a sea of gin and red wine! Driving my friends away, taking up with whoever was left in a Paris bar at three in the morning! It didn't work. She says my drinking and a Hollywood starlet drove her to ballet? I say Jozan and her ballet drove me to drink. Now she says give up drink and all will be fine with us? Are you so naive or so stupid as to actually believe that to be true? Me paranoid? What about last time? She was at the Clinic on my dime, and in three weeks she produced her first novel!

RENTON

Six weeks.

SCOTT

I don't care how many weeks! I labour for months, for years, planning, refining. Writing. With hackwork to pay for her care sucking me dry. And she writes a novel in six weeks? Her incoming and outgoing mail censored at the Clinic, and she sends Scribners a manuscript! How did that happen?

RENTON

We're not entirely sure.

SCOTT

Perhaps a member of staff delivered it for her.

RENTON

Most unlikely.

SCOTT

Maybe you delivered it for her.

RENTON

I did not.

SCOTT

Maybe it arrived on angel's wings! Scribners accepts it. Isn't that wonderful? Isn't that just bloody fantastic!? Scribners publishes her novel, and what is that novel about? Our life. Our life together and thinly, thinly disguised. While I myself am writing a novel based on the same raw material and experience!

RENTON

The Clinic's apologized. I've apologized. What else can we do?

SCOTT

You can listen to what I'm telling you now.

RENTON

Isn't Scribners your publisher? Why didn't you ask them to withdraw their offer to Zelda?

SCOTT

How could I do that to her? I would never do that to her! How could you think that I would?

RENTON
Why not?

SCOTT
I could not do that to her!

RENTON
Look, I know her desire to write still exists. I know this concerns you.

SCOTT
Her competitive compulsion is diagnosed as a symptom of illness! The manifestation it takes – first dancing, now writing! Of course it concerns me!

RENTON
That diagnosis seems – convenient – for you.

SCOTT
You are a bastard – but I suppose hundreds of people have called you that.

RENTON
I wish my practice were that large.

SCOTT
And ambitious too. You're ambitious.

RENTON
I've told you I don't doubt your concern. You're obviously deeply concerned that your wife may be at work on a novel. I emphasize "may be." Your concern is so great you perceive that possibility as reality. That's all there is to it. She is not writing. You're afraid that she's writing.

SCOTT
She's in her room for hours with the door locked, refusing to eat, exercise, or follow the clearly agreed upon schedule of activities set by your own psychiatric clinic! She rejects the role of wife or mother! She refuses to interact with either Scotty or me! What do you think she's doing in there?

I'll tell you. She is obsessively covering reams of paper with sprawling sights and sounds and smells and incoherent thoughts scrawled across each page in soft lead pencil! And concealing it from me!

And you, you next thing I know will smuggle out a manuscript to Scribners or some disreputable publisher only too happy to feed the public's maw with life as viewed through the shattered lens of America's former foremost literary figure's better half! My wife.

RENTON
If Zelda's new work, supposing it exists, is so disorganized who would publish it anyway? While you

SCOTT

Do you think good writing guarantees publication? Or bad writing blocks it? Quality has nothing to do with it. Scott Fitzgerald is out of style! He crawls for crumbs like a mouse under Hollywood's table while the rats make deals!

ZELDA

(She slips off the chair onto the floor facing the audience.) Yes the rats make deals and when Ernest Hemingway opens his mouth I want to say Bullshit! *(emphasizing her "bullshit" banging both hands on the floor)* I want my hearing and knowing his Bullshit to count! I want to be there Full In my Own Skin! I want my words to count because they're mine and I count!

SCOTT

A great literary talent, do you hear what she calls him?

ZELDA

My words don't count except when he steals them.

SCOTT

She calls it bullshit and him bogus.

ZELDA

(up off the floor and turning on SCOTT) He calls you a fool and a hopeless drunk. I call you a bootlicker and more.

SCOTT

Much more.

ZELDA

Or less.

SCOTT

Say it. Get it out there in the open. Thanks to you it's whispered about.

ZELDA

I wasn't the first. Robert McAlmon was first but you prefer to pretend it was me.

SCOTT

Tell him what you said about Ernest and me.

ZELDA

When I ask you to come to bed you tell me I should sleep with the janitor or the man who delivers the coal!

SCOTT

A homosexual liaison between Ernest and me.

ZELDA
I said please please!

SCOTT
Defiling forever that sincere love and respect that existed between Ernest and me.

ZELDA
I said why don't you want to?

SCOTT
Destroyed our friendship forever!

ZELDA
What is it, what's wrong?

SCOTT
Destroyed any chance of open spontaneous comradeship with others forever!

ZELDA
I said I was desperately unhappy

SCOTT
I place my hand under a friend's elbow when we hit a slippery spot in the rain?

ZELDA
I said

SCOTT
I quickly withdraw my hand.

ZELDA
I said that's the why of Jozan!

SCOTT
Fill the awkward space with banal commentary on the vagaries of Parisian weather! That's what she's done with her unjust indictment of Ernest and me!

ZELDA
Bullshit!

SCOTT
You may keep that retort. It's worthless to me. "Bull Shit" Those words are yours.

ZELDA
Bullshit bullshit bullshit!

SCOTT
All yours.

ZELDA
Bullshit!

SCOTT
Do you know what I gave up for her?

ZELDA
Bullshit bullshit

SCOTT
When I married her what I gave up?

ZELDA
Tell me go on tell me tell me!

> *ZELDA hits the straight-backed chair sending it flying. RENTON grabs it and moves it out of harm's way.*

SCOTT
Other Women! The pleasure of other women! Do you have any awareness of the number of beautiful and desirable women a literary figure attracts? Celebrity status attracts? I attract? Do you? I gave that up, all of that up, for her!

For you. When I married you I gave all of that up! Fidelity meant something to me!

ZELDA
I never asked you for that.

SCOTT
Out of her own mouth, a fine example of her moral turpitude.

Marriage, Zelda! Vows that were taken? Or did you think that ceremony was just another cheap theatrical piece you were performing for friends?

ZELDA
What friends? There was nobody there but my sisters.

SCOTT
Ludlow Fowler was there!

ZELDA
Correction! My sisters and Ludlow Fowler were there.

SCOTT

You never believed in me or my writing! *(to RENTON)* Refused to marry me till the publishers' checks started coming!

ZELDA

I drew sketches of Gatsby till my fingers ached, so you could see the man clear in your mind! "Revisions with Zelda" "Revising with Zelda" Isn't that what you said to Ober and Perkins?

SCOTT

So we collaborate now?

ZELDA

No.

SCOTT

Isn't that what you're saying?

ZELDA

No!

SCOTT

The literary achievement of Scott Fitzgerald is the result of collaboration with his crazy wife Zelda!

ZELDA

No!

SCOTT

That's what she wants the world to believe!

ZELDA

I contribute!

SCOTT

Nothing!

ZELDA

Something!

SCOTT

Nothing! The money! That's all it ever meant to you. I'm caught in a descending spiral churning out short stories putting aside major work and for what?

ZELDA

For another gin and no mix!

SCOTT

For you! To keep you in treatment, that's what!

ZELDA
  I don't ask to be treated!

SCOTT
  Where you have time and opportunity to indulge yourself on paper while my
  time is spent grinding out grist for the magazine mill and the movies!

ZELDA
  I'm disciplined and I c-concentrate!

SCOTT
  You have a manic obsession!

ZELDA
  I marshal my f-forces!

SCOTT
  A manic obsession! First you think you're a dancer! Now you think you're a
  writer!

ZELDA
  I need to Do Something!

SCOTT
  You don't need to Do Something! You just want to Be Someone! There's a
  difference you know!

  Pause.

ZELDA
  I thought, I was a salamander once. I thought I could live, in fire.

  He tells me I'm nothing. I'm an impediment. An encumbrance.

  I need to find out which of these stories is true.

SCOTT
  (exhausted) Can't you grasp the simple fact that Scotty needs to be educated
  and fed? That there is a household such as it is, to maintain?

ZELDA
  (and she is exhausted) You're always there.

SCOTT
  Now what are you saying?

ZELDA
  Scotty.

SCOTT
What about Scotty?

ZELDA
You're there.

SCOTT
Where?

ZELDA
There's no room for me at the table.

SCOTT
What, when we eat? There's plenty of room at the table. Your place is set. Why aren't you in it?

ZELDA
I wanted a boy.

SCOTT
A beautiful little girl. She wanted a boy.

ZELDA
She was born, and I said, words. I think that's why he was there, so he could fling a net, pull them in, swallow them whole and later push them down "Daisy's" throat with his tongue... and when "Daisy" speaks... words stolen out of my mouth. She's always present tense, and me? Always past, words disappear into air, snatched away do you know what I mean? I wanted to call her Patricia.

SCOTT
Her name is Frances Scott Fitzgerald.

ZELDA
Pat.

SCOTT
Her name is Scotty.

ZELDA
He's always teaching her something he's reading her something

SCOTT
It's what fathers do, Zelda!

ZELDA
(She begins to turn round and round in the same spot.) He hires her nannies oversees her studies teaches her chess decides which sport what class whose friends what time he's a very good father!

SCOTT

> She has no mother!

ZELDA

> Poor Thing! *(turning faster and faster, pounding the air with her fists)*
> Pooooorthiiing!

SCOTT

> Zelda! *(moving to stop her)*

RENTON

> Let her go. Let her go! Leave her.

> *SCOTT turns to RENTON. ZELDA will gradually stop on her own.*

SCOTT

> Let. Her. Go. Let her go…. And where would she like to go, doctor? A public institution? Which will be all I can afford if things aren't resolved!

> Would you like to go there, Zelda? That snake pit for crazies?

ZELDA

> No no not – Like an oyster, you know, like an oyster?

SCOTT

> *(to RENTON)* See what you've started?

ZELDA

> Everything's gone. Those things that you said were inside? They're all gone now. The glorious glorious Glory? Inside? It's gone. Empty. Shucked from my shell, hollow inside. What do I fill it with now?

SCOTT

> *(sits)* Here we go.

ZELDA

> Somebody tell me!

SCOTT

> That's enough.

ZELDA

> The bitterness and the anger inside, can you take that away?

RENTON

> Zelda.

ZELDA
And replace it with what, tell me what? You don't know with what! He doesn't know! Nobody knows! *(She retreats.)*

SCOTT
Now… Doctor… Renton, now… you… you will do… you will do as I say.

RENTON
I will do, what is called for.

SCOTT
And I will tell you what is called for. Zelda?

RENTON
What is medically called for!

SCOTT
You will back my position. Do you want to know why? *(gently)* Zelda?

ZELDA
(a spiritual discovery is beginning to fill the "empty inside") God will come. If you call, He will come

SCOTT
Is the doctor writing?

ZELDA
I called. You. Yes, yes I did

SCOTT
Is the doctor writing a book? A book, Zelda, like you told me before?

RENTON
The answer is no.

ZELDA
(talking to SCOTT, referring to SCOTT as God) "Do Do" I called you.

SCOTT
Is he writing?

RENTON
We've settled that question!

ZELDA
And they said what does that mean "Dieu Dieu" why do you call Him that?

SCOTT
Just answer me Zelda.

RENTON

For God's sake leave her alone!

ZELDA

(kneeling, clasping SCOTT's hand) I call you God, and I'm calling you God, and I'm asking you to let me go Dieu.

SCOTT

Does he run little errands?

RENTON

No.

ZELDA

Please fill me with something. Send voices and visions and You can take all the words!

SCOTT

Did he deliver your novel?

RENTON

The answer is no!

ZELDA

I don't care you can have them.

SCOTT

Yes, Zelda?

ZELDA

I'll write in tongues and no one will hear.

> *ZELDA begins speaking in tongues, a low murmur, running the words together, pressing SCOTT's hand to her cheek. It's actually a list of the Parisian bars in which SCOTT and she drank.*

Deux Magots Closerie des Lilas Lipp's Coupole Dome MontmartreSelect Trianon Ciro's Foyot la Reine Pedauque

SCOTT

She says the answer is yes.

RENTON

Why

ZELDA

(continuing to speak under the men's dialogue) Trianon Ciro's Foyot la Reine Pedauque Bricktop's Zelli's le Perroquet Maxim's Crillon the Ritz Deux Magots Closerie des Lilas Lipp's Coupole Dome MontmartreSelect Trianon Ciro's Foyot

la Reine Pedauque Bricktop's Zelli's le Perroquet Maxim's Crillon the Ritz Deux
Magots Closerie des Lilas Lipp's Coupole Dome MontmartreSelect Trianon
Ciro's Foyot la Reine Pedauque Bricktop's Zelli's le Perroquet Maxim's Crillon
the Ritz Deux Magots Closerie des Lilas Lipp's Coupole

RENTON
Why are you doing this?

SCOTT
(*extricates himself from ZELDA's grasp*) There will be no more of her "artistic
expression," most particularly none in the literary field, unless I approve.

RENTON
And control?

SCOTT
Painting. She likes painting. She can paint what she likes. But her literary
indulgence is a prelude to breakdown. Is that your analysis, doctor? (*pause*) Or
would you prefer to pursue your career in a state-run snake pit, instead of the
prestigious and private Phipps clinic?

RENTON
Why?

SCOTT
You say that you listen, but do you actually hear?

RENTON
I can see. Look at her! Look what you're doing!

SCOTT
What I'm doing. What am I doing? I tell you over and over what I am doing
and why I am doing it. I am fighting for the Material Survival, of the Fitzgerald
Menage, Cracked and Crazed as its Members Might Be!

ZELDA's murmur is dying away.

Believe that! And… and for the one thing, that in the end really matters…. The
Writing.

I am writing! Because I'm a Writer! I am writing a novel!

ZELDA
It's my fault he didn't make the football team at Princeton I know that!

SCOTT
An intensely personal novel, one in which psychiatry and psychiatric material
play a predominant role!

ZELDA
Was never president of the triangle Triangle Club!

SCOTT
She's taken research material belonging to me, didn't you Zelda?

ZELDA
He never married Ginevra King! Never led his men over hills to kill Huns!

SCOTT
That's how I knew.

ZELDA
My fault!

SCOTT
Knew she was writing and mining the same seam of personal experience and research as I am. Again!

ZELDA
My fault?

SCOTT
Just like before!

ZELDA
(She's working herself into a violent attack on him, trying to find a way, in self-defense, to penetrate his defenses.) My fault you always feel poor among rich? Not as bright among brilliant?

SCOTT
You promised, after your novel, the publication of which I did not prevent, you promised you would concentrate on your painting!

ZELDA
Is that my fault?!

SCOTT
I want to hear you agree to that today!

ZELDA
Is it my fault you need to be noticed! And to do what you need to do to be noticed, you need to be drunk!

SCOTT
(to RENTON) Why can't you see what I'm up against?

l to r: Daniel Arnold, Maev Beatty, Trevor Leigh.

ZELDA

Not a nice drunk! A nasty obnoxious obstreperous drunk! And then when you're drunk you're unable to write! That is not my fault!

SCOTT

Life with you necessitates drink. It's a means of survival!

ZELDA

I Can write! And I Will write! Because I keep at it and on it and do it! And you cannot forgive me for that!

> *She has wounded him. He moves away to get a drink; she follows him wanting to deal a mortal blow physically and psychologically. He can't get away from her.*

Is it my fault your father was nothing!
A failure!
A pretentious and poor Irish clerk!
Who lived off your mother!
Went on discreet Irish binges!
Drunk in the yard!
Trying to play ball with his son!
Falling down drunk!
Neighbours at windows! Laughing! Yes laughing and pointing and!!

SCOTT

(grabs her wrists stopping her physical and verbal assault) EE-Nough!! *(pause)*
The last time you mentioned my father,
I bloodied your nose,
and blackened your eye
and your sister did go home in a cab.
You hurt me.
I hit you.
I want you to know, that at this moment, you have inflicted, no pain. No Pain,
I feel…. Absolutely No Pain…. None at all.

> *SCOTT releases her wrists, gets his drink. Pause. He takes in RENTON. He speaks conversationally almost as if he were picking up where a prior friendly and informal conversation had left off. He ignores ZELDA.*

You know… I told Edmund once—my friend?—Edmund Wilson? I told him, near my beginning… before the beginning… that I had a dream. I wanted Scott Fitzgerald to be one of the greatest writers that ever lived. I suppose he thought I was a bit of a fool. A young fool. "One of the greatest writers that ever lived." I meant it.

I met Zelda
And we have continued. On.
From there.

He looks at ZELDA, an objective cold scrutiny.

When you attacked my friendship with Ernest, we were in Paris on the Rue Palatine. Do you remember? It was raining. For the first time I entertained the notion of leaving you. It entered my cerebrum stage right. Did a very slow waltz. And exited left.

I found it most entertaining.

ZELDA
I will write! With this*!*

> *Her hand to heart. Her actions will grow increasingly violent as she mounts an attack on herself.*

And this! *(clutches her stomach)*
And this! *(both arms embrace herself)*
And these! *(strikes her legs and falls to her knees)*
And this! And this! And this!*(holds both her hands out and up, hitting at herself)*
What these have seen and heard! *(her eyes and ears)*

> *SCOTT gets behind her, wrapping his arms around her, gently, struggling to restrain her.*

And what has come from here! *(her mouth)*
While splintered shards of meaning

> *Striking her head with both hands, flailing at herself as SCOTT struggles to hold her, speaking softly under her words, crooning to her as if she were a baby, while she continues over his words.*

turn and twist in here but sometimes still and beautiful! Muddled! Disjointed! Out of tune and out of time you tell me but it's all I have to Shape and Mold! What else can I make something from, but this Poor Thing? It's all I have, why can't I? It's mine! Why not?

Why not, you tell me why!

SCOTT
There there, there there, it's all right, yes, yes it is, it's all right Zelda.

> *SCOTT is somewhat successful in his efforts to calm her. As he rocks her gently back and forth her physical assault on herself stops.*

ZELDA
Why not?

SCOTT
It's all right. *(whispers)* I love you. You hear me, Zelda? I love you.

ZELDA
> Hear you.

SCOTT
> I love you.

ZELDA
> Love me.

SCOTT
> I'll never leave you.

ZELDA
> Leave me no.

SCOTT
> Care for you. Love you.

ZELDA
> Love you.

SCOTT
> Helpmate to me. I need you. And mother to Scotty. That's health and happiness, Zelda. The doctors say that. I say that. And you know that.

ZELDA
> Yes.... Yes. But... why not?

> *Pause.*

SCOTT
> Why. Not. *(gets up from the floor)* Why not.... Why not? *(pause)*

Because. Because you... you... are a third rate writer, with nothing to say... and I, I am a writer of some talent and genius, As Assessed By Others, not myself. Our lives, and all that that entails, before and since we met, and what can be made from them, belong to me.

> *Pause. ZELDA lies on the floor where the red slipper and skull-like fragment of sculpture lay at the beginning. She is not defeated, she is regrouping. SCOTT becomes aware of RENTON. He interprets RENTON's steady gaze as criticism.*

I speak the truth. *(pause)*

You can dismiss, if you want, my work's literary merit, what I've achieved or not, or have yet to achieve or not. I'll make it simple. Three people are completely dependent on me. Roof over their heads, food on the table, clothes on their backs, Zelda's treatment, Scotty's education, my own basic needs. Do you think Zelda is capable of providing even for herself? *(pause)* Do you?

RENTON
Perhaps. In time. Away from you.

SCOTT
But I love her. And she loves me. Didn't you hear her?… If you didn't why don't you ask her? *(pause)*

She – she spoke of, my father. My father… my, poor, Irish father. He didn't pass on much, but, a sense of honor and obligation.

I will never abandon Zelda.
I will never abdicate responsibility for Scotty.
It's me who provides. I am the wage earner. The one worth preserving for that reason alone. And my work is my writing, is my art. And I claim, yes I do, I claim exclusive ownership of the raw material from which my art springs.

I've paid for it, with Pain…. Anguish…. Regretted Actions…. Faded Visions, Depleted Hope, Impoverished Dreams…. Too much Gin…. Some Joy… and Endless Practice of the Craft since Childhood.

And if you find fault with my, reasoning, then you and I must part company, with, I'm afraid, an unfortunate, perhaps disastrous, effect on your career… trajectory.

RENTON
Which is it, a threat or blackmail?

SCOTT
It could be construed as either, if one were paranoid. Or had something to hide.

ZELDA is entering another reality. She is not present for SCOTT and RENTON.

ZELDA
Momma *(getting up, her red slippers have come off and are on the floor)* I'm not afraid to die.

RENTON
Dr. Gebhardt would rub your nose in it.

SCOTT
Perhaps that's why I'm talking to you.

ZELDA speaks without sorrow. The details of SCOTT's death in a crass and commercial Hollywood, his lack of discipline re his writing, the alcoholic's craving for sweets; his sophomoric obsession with Princeton, give her a sense of personal victory.

ZELDA
Scott first. In a Hollywood apartment. Putting his writing aside, eating a chocolate bar, while reading the football news from Princeton. His fluttering heart? Like a sparrow in a bully's fist. Stopped.

SCOTT
(acknowledges LAHEURSA directly for the first time) Close with this. She will not indulge in artistic endeavors without my express consent.

LAHEURSA will not record any more of ZELDA's words.

ZELDA
I'm not afraid to die.

SCOTT
And my recommendations for institutional recommitment or release will be acted upon.

LAHEURSA records these words. Faint sound of wind and flame. LAHEURSA will remove the sheet of paper from the machine and place the sheet on top of the pile of paper on the desk. She will put on her cloak and hat.

Do we have an understanding, Doctor?

ZELDA
I Will die.

SCOTT
Doctor?

ZELDA
(an ecstatic vision of the future) Highland Hospital. Top floor. Doors locked. Windows barred. Six women consumed by fire. Zelda Sayre. Fitzgerald. Identified by a slipper that lies beneath some bones. Realized at last! Transformed! Transcendent in the flames!

RENTON
The transcript?

SCOTT
Belongs to me. With signatures, of course.

SCOTT holds out a pen to RENTON. The men are still.

Oct. 30/07

ZELDA

Through the shackled window I see a pair of stockings hung on the clothesline in the outside porch. As I burn, I see, in the light and wind of the flames, I see the stockings dance!

> *LAHEURSA picks up the pile of paper. She approaches ZELDA and gives her the papers. The sound of "The Dance of the Wooden Soldiers" slightly distorted as at the beginning of the play creeps in and will grow in volume as wind and flame fade out.*

> *ZELDA looks at the first page, it drifts to the floor, similarly so the second. All of the manuscript pages slowly rain from ZELDA's hands down onto the red slippers as music grows in volume.*

> *In the background RENTON takes the pen, and lights fade to black.*

> *The end.*